Scrap Quilts Galore

Oxmoor House®

Contents

Workshop	4
Pinwheel	12
Flying Under Radar	14
Windmills	17
Arkansas Crossroads	20
Double Wedding Ring	22
3-D Nine-Patch	26
Roads	30
Memory Chain	33
Texas Star	36
Maple Leaf	40
Wandering Star	43
My Charming Star	46

SCRAP QUILTS GALORE

From the *Quilts Made Easy®* series
©1996 by Oxmoor House, Inc.

Book Division of Southern Progress Corporation
P.O. Box 2463, Birmingham, AL 35201

Published by Oxmoor House, Inc., and Leisure Arts, Inc.

All rights reserved. No part of this book may be reproduced in any form or by any means without the prior written permission of the publisher, excepting brief quotations in connection with reviews written specifically for inclusion in magazines or newspapers.

Library of Congress Catalog Number: 95-73263
ISBN: 0-8487-1285-4

Manufactured in the United States of America
Fifth Printing 1999

Quilts Made Easy® is a federally registered trademark of Oxmoor House, Inc.

Editor-in-Chief: Nancy Fitzpatrick Wyatt
Editorial Director, Special Interest Publications: Ann H. Harvey
Senior Crafts Editor: Susan Ramey Cleveland
Senior Editor, Editorial Services: Olivia Kindig Wells
Art Director: James Boone

SCRAP QUILTS GALORE

Editor: Linda Baltzell Wright
Editorial Assistant: Barzella Estle
Copy Editor: Jennifer K. Mathews
Senior Designer: Larry Hunter
Designer: Carol Loria
Illustrator: Kelly Davis
Publishing Systems Administrator: Rick Tucker
Senior Photographer: John O'Hagan
Photo Stylist: Katie Stoddard
Production and Distribution Director: Phillip Lee
Associate Production Managers: Theresa L. Beste, Vanessa D. Cobbs
Production Coordinator: Marianne Jordan Wilson
Production Assistant: Valerie Heard

Dear Quilting Friends,

Fabric is the essense of quilting. It's why we love the process so—the colors, the textures, the designs, the emotions that a particular print can conjure. Who among us doesn't love running her hands over the luscious bolts of cloth in the fabric store. And who doesn't own a collection of these treasured textiles? The "scrap bag" of today's quilter is often several shelves or boxes full of fabric pieces—or, in at least one case I know of, a whole room devoted to the stuff.

In the following pages, you'll find 12 wonderful designs in which to use your fabric treasures. From the stately *Maple Leaf* on page 40, made by members of the Birmingham Quilters Guild, to Pepper Cory's Drunkard's Path interpretation, *Flying Under Radar*, on page 14, these designs will inspire you to delve into the depths of your fabric stash and come up with the makings of a beautiful quilt.

You might choose the simplicity of Lorraine Vignoli's *My Charming Star* on page 46 or Alvida Baltzell's *Windmills* on page 17. Or you might be looking for a challenge such as you'll find in Mary Ramey's *Double Wedding Ring* on page 22. Whatever your quilting skill, inspiration awaits you in the pages of this book.

Happy stitching,

Susan Ramey Cleveland

WORKSHOP

Selecting Fabrics

The best fabric for quilts is 100% cotton. Yardage requirements are based on 44"-wide fabric and allow for shrinkage. All fabrics, including backing, should be machine-washed, dried, and pressed before cutting. Use warm water and detergent but not fabric softener.

Necessary Notions

- Scissors
- Rotary cutter and mat
- Acrylic rulers
- Template plastic
- Pencils for marking cutting lines
- Sewing needles
- Sewing thread
- Sewing machine
- Seam ripper
- Pins
- Iron and ironing board
- Quilting needles
- Thimble
- Hand quilting thread
- Machine quilting thread

Making Templates

A template is a duplication of a printed pattern, made from a sturdy material, which is traced onto fabric. Many regular shapes such as squares and triangles can be marked directly on the fabric with a ruler, but you need templates for other shapes. Some quiltmakers use templates for all shapes.

You can trace patterns directly onto template plastic. Or make a template by tracing a pattern onto graph paper and gluing the paper to posterboard or sandpaper. (Sandpaper will not slip on fabric.)

When a large pattern is given in two pieces, make one template for the complete piece.

Cut out the template on the marked line. It is important that a template be traced, marked, and cut accurately. If desired, punch out corner dots with a ⅛"-diameter hole punch (**Diagram 1**).

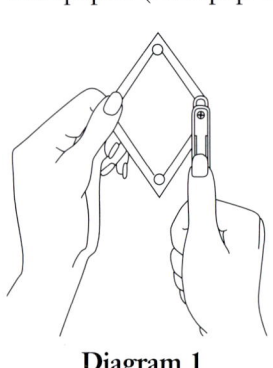
Diagram 1

Mark each template with its letter and grain line. Verify the template's accuracy, placing it over the printed pattern. Any discrepancy, however small, is multiplied many times as the quilt is assembled. Another way to check templates' accuracy is to make a test block before cutting more pieces.

Tracing Templates on Fabric

For hand piecing, templates should be cut to the finished size of the piece so seam lines can be marked on the fabric. Avoiding the selvage, place the template *facedown* on the *wrong* side of the fabric, aligning the template grain line with the straight grain. Hold the template firmly and trace around it. Repeat as needed, leaving ½" between tracings (**Diagram 2**).

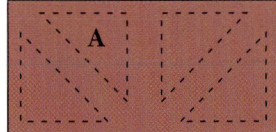
Diagram 2

For machine piecing, templates should include seam allowances. These templates are used in the same manner as for hand piecing, but you can mark the fabric using common lines for efficient cutting (**Diagram 3**). Mark corners on fabric through holes in the template.

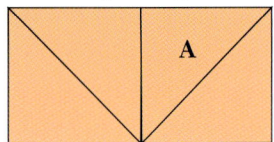
Diagram 3

For hand or machine piecing, use window templates to enhance accuracy by drawing and cutting out both cutting and sewing lines. The guidance of a drawn seam line is very useful for sewing set-in seams, when pivoting at a precise point is critical. Used on the right side of the fabric, window templates help you cut specific motifs with accuracy (**Diagram 4**).

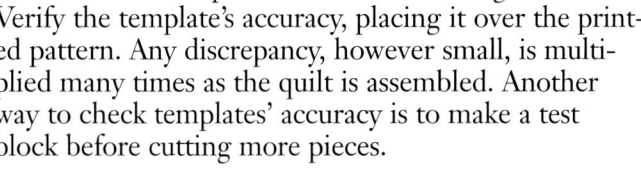
Diagram 4

For hand appliqué, templates should be made the finished size. Place templates *faceup* on the *right* side of the fabric. Position tracings at least ½" apart (**Diagram 5**). Add a ¼" seam allowance around pieces when cutting.

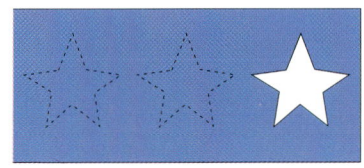
Diagram 5

Cutting

Grain Lines

Woven threads form the fabric's grain. Lengthwise grain, parallel to the selvages, has the least stretch; crosswise grain has a little more give.

Long strips such as borders should be cut lengthwise whenever possible and cut first to ensure that you have the necessary length. Usually, other pieces can be cut aligned with either grain.

Bias is the 45° diagonal line between the two grain directions. Bias has the most stretch and is used for curving strips such as flower stems. Bias is often preferred for binding.

Never use the selvage (finished edge). Selvage does not react to washing, drying, and pressing like the rest of the fabric and may pucker when the finished quilt is laundered.

Rotary Cutting

A rotary cutter, used with a protective mat and a ruler, takes getting used to but is very efficient for cutting strips, squares, and triangles. A rotary cutter is fast because you can measure and cut multiple layers with a single stroke, without templates or marking. It is also more accurate than cutting with scissors because fabrics remain flat and do not move during cutting.

Because the blade is very sharp, be sure to get a rotary cutter with a safety guard. Keep the guard in the safe position at all times, except when making a cut. *Always keep the cutter out of the reach of children.*

Use the cutter with a self-healing mat. A good mat for cutting strips is at least 23" wide.

1. Squaring the fabric is the first step in accurate cutting. Fold the fabric with selvages aligned. With the yardage to your right, align a small square ruler with the fold near the cut edge. Place a long ruler against the left side of the square (**Diagram 6**). Keeping the long ruler in place, remove the square. Hold the ruler in place with your left hand as you cut, rolling the cutter *away from you* along the ruler's edge with a steady motion. You can move your left hand along the ruler as you cut, but do not change the position of the ruler. *Keep your fingers away from the ruler's edge when cutting.*

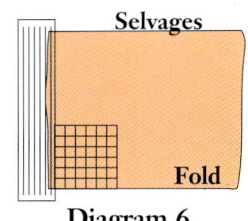
Diagram 6

2. Open the fabric. If the cut was not accurately perpendicular to the fold, the edge will be V-shaped instead of straight (**Diagram 7**). Correct the cut if necessary.

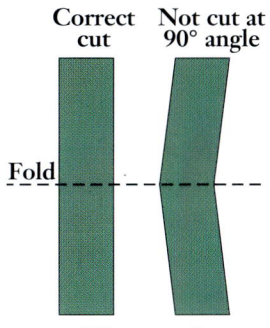
Diagram 7

3. With a transparent ruler, you can measure and cut at the same time. Fold the fabric in half again, aligning the selvages with the fold, making four layers that line up perfectly along the cut edge. Project instructions designate the strip width needed. Position the ruler to measure the correct distance from the edge (**Diagram 8**) and cut. The blade will easily cut through all four layers. Check the strip to be sure the cut is straight. The strip length is the width of the fabric, approximately 43" to 44". Using the ruler again, trim selvages, cutting about ⅜" from each end.

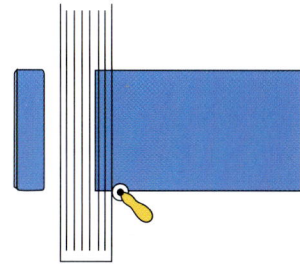
Diagram 8

4. To cut squares and rectangles from a strip, align the desired measurement on the ruler with the strip end and cut across the strip (**Diagram 9**).

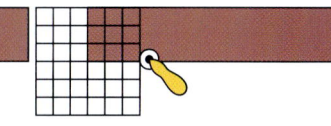
Diagram 9

5. Cut triangles from squares or rectangles. Cutting instructions often direct you to cut a square in half or in quarters diagonally to make right triangles, and this technique can apply to rectangles, too (**Diagram 10**). The outside edges of the square or rectangle are on the straight of the grain, so triangle sides cut on the diagonal are bias.

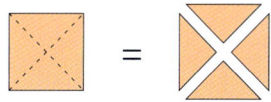

Diagram 10

6. Some projects in this book use a time-saving technique called strip piecing. With this method, strips are joined to make a pieced band. Cut across the seams of this band to cut preassembled units (**Diagram 11**).

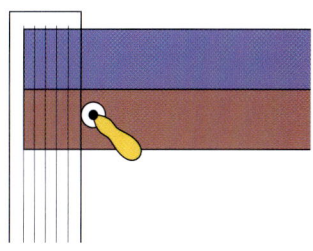
Diagram 11

Machine Piecing

Your sewing machine does not have to be a new, computerized model. A good straight stitch is all that's necessary, but it may be helpful to have a nice satin stitch for appliqué. Clean and oil your machine regularly, use good-quality thread, and replace needles frequently.

1. Patches for machine piecing are cut with the seam allowance included, but the sewing line is not usually marked. Therefore, a way to make a consistent ¼" seam is essential. Some presser feet have a right toe that is ¼" from the needle. Other machines have an adjustable needle that can be set for a ¼" seam. If your machine has neither feature, experiment to find how the fabric must be placed to make a ¼" seam. Mark this position on the presser foot or throat plate.

2. Use a stitch length that makes a strong seam but is not too difficult to remove with a seam ripper. The best setting is usually 10 to 12 stitches per inch.

3. Pin only when really necessary. If a straight seam is less than 4" and does not have to match an adjoining seam, pinning is not necessary.

4. When intersecting seams must align (**Diagram 12**), match the units with right sides facing and push a pin through both seams at the seam line. Turn the pinned unit to the right side to check the alignment; then pin securely. As you sew, remove each pin just before the needle reaches it.

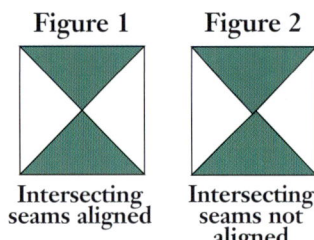

Diagram 12

5. Block assembly diagrams are used throughout this book to show how pieces should be joined. Make small units first; then join them in rows and continue joining rows to finish the block (**Diagram 13**). Blocks are joined in the same manner to complete the quilt top.

6. Chain piecing saves time. Stack pieces to be sewn in pairs, with right sides facing. Join the first pair as usual. At the end of the seam, do not backstitch, cut the thread, or lift the presser foot. Just feed in the next pair of pieces—the machine will make a few stitches between pieces before the needle strikes the second piece of fabric. Continue sewing in this way until all pairs are joined. Stack the chain of pieces until you are ready to clip them apart (**Diagram 14**).

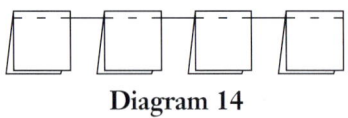

Diagram 14

7. Most seams are sewn straight across, from raw edge to raw edge. Since they will be crossed by other seams, they do not require backstitching to secure them.

8. When piecing diamonds or other angled seams, you may need to make set-in seams. For these, always mark the corner dots (shown on the patterns) on the fabric pieces. Stitch one side, starting at the outside edge and being careful not to sew beyond the dot into the seam allowance (**Diagram 15, Figure A**). Backstitch. Align the other side of the piece as needed, with right sides facing. Sew from the dot to the outside edge (**Figure B**).

9. Sewing curved seams requires extra care. First, mark the centers of both the convex (outward) and concave (inward) curves (**Diagram 16**). Staystitch just inside the seam allowance of both pieces. Clip the concave piece to the stitching (**Figure A**). With right sides facing and raw edges aligned, pin the two patches together at the center (**Figure B**) and at the left edge (**Figure C**). Sew from edge to center, stopping frequently to check that the raw edges are aligned. Stop at the center with the needle down. Raise the presser foot and pin the pieces together from the center to the right edge. Lower the foot and continue to sew. Press seam allowances toward the concave curve (**Figure D**).

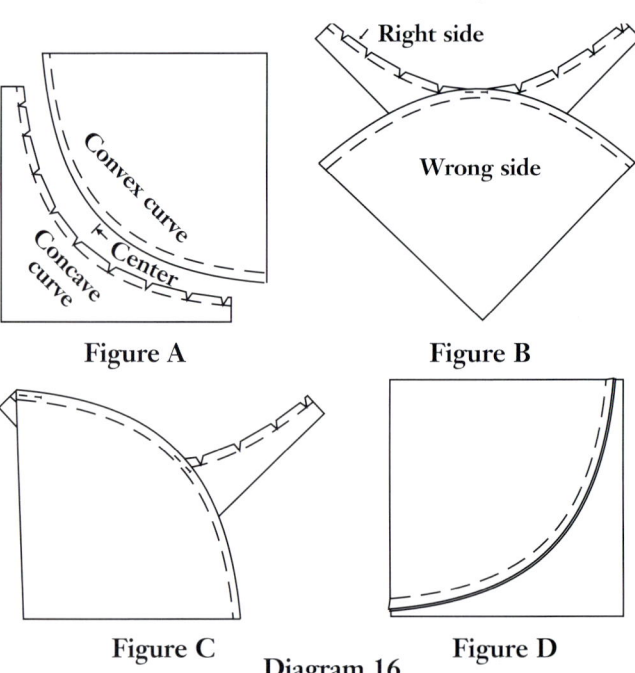

Diagram 16

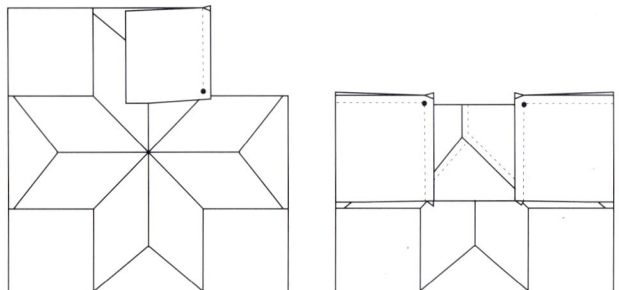

Diagram 15

Hand Piecing

Make a running stitch of 8 to 10 stitches per inch along the marked seam line on the wrong side of the fabric. Don't pull the fabric as you sew; let the pieces lie relaxed in your hand. Sew from seam line to seam line, not from edge to edge as in machine piecing.

When ending a line of stitching, backstitch over the last stitch and make a loop knot **(Diagram 17)**.

Match seams and points accurately, pinning patches together before piecing. Align match points as described in Step 4 under Machine Piecing.

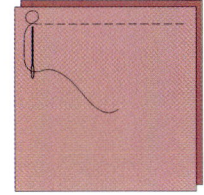
Diagram 17

When joining units where several seams meet, do not sew over seam allowances; sew *through* them at the match point **(Diagram 18)**. When four or more seams meet, press the seam allowances in the same direction to reduce bulk **(Diagram 19)**.

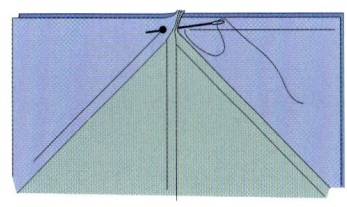
Diagram 18

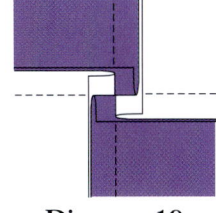
Diagram 19

Pressing

Careful pressing is necessary for precise piecing. Press each seam as you go. Sliding the iron back and forth may push the seam out of shape. Use an up-and-down motion, lifting the iron from spot to spot. Press the seam flat on the wrong side. Open the piece and, on the right side, press both seam allowances to one side (usually toward the darker fabric). Pressing the seam open leaves tiny gaps through which batting may beard.

Appliqué

Traditional Hand Appliqué

Hand appliqué requires that you turn under a seam allowance around the shape to prevent frayed edges.

1. Trace around the template on the right side of the fabric. This line indicates where to turn the seam allowance. Cut each piece approximately ¼" outside the line.

2. For simple shapes, turn the edges by pressing the seam allowance to the back; complex shapes may require basting the seam allowance. Sharp points and strong curves are best appliquéd with freezer paper. Clip curves to make a smooth edge. With practice, you can work without pressing seam allowances, turning edges under with the needle as you sew.

3. Do not turn under any seam allowance that will be covered by another appliqué piece.

4. To stitch, use one strand of cotton-wrapped polyester sewing thread in a color that matches the appliqué. Use a slipstitch, but keep the stitch very small on the surface. Working from right to left (or left to right if you're left-handed), pull the needle through the base fabric and catch only a few threads on the folded edge of the appliqué. Reinsert the needle into the base fabric, under the top thread on the appliqué edge to keep the thread from tangling **(Diagram 20)**.

5. An alternative to slipstitching is to work a decorative buttonhole stitch around each figure **(Diagram 21)**.

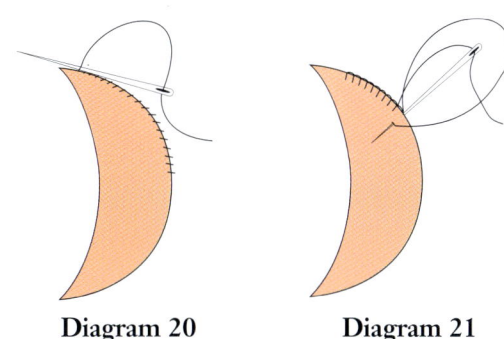
Diagram 20   Diagram 21

Freezer Paper Hand Appliqué

Supermarket freezer paper saves time because it eliminates the need for basting seam allowances.

1. Trace the template onto the *dull* side of the freezer paper and cut the paper on the marked line. *Note:* If a design is not symmetrical, turn the template over and trace a mirror image so the fabric piece won't be reversed when you cut it out.

2. Pin the freezer-paper shape, with its *shiny side* up, to the *wrong side* of the fabric. Following the paper shape and adding a scant ¼" seam allowance, cut out the fabric piece. Do not remove pins.

3. Using just the tip of a dry iron, press the seam allowance to the shiny side of the paper. Be careful not to touch the freezer paper with the iron.

4. Appliqué the piece to the background as in traditional appliqué. Trim the fabric from behind the shape, leaving ¼" seam allowances. Separate the freezer paper from the fabric with your fingernail and pull gently to remove it. If you prefer not to trim the background fabric, pull out the freezer paper before you complete stitching.

5. Sharp points require special attention. Turn the point down and press it **(Diagram 22, Figure A)**. Fold the seam allowance on one side over the point and press **(Figure B)**; then fold the other seam allowance over the point and press **(Figure C)**.

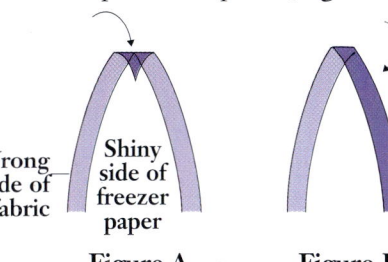
Wrong side of fabric | Shiny side of freezer paper

Figure A   Figure B   Figure C

Diagram 22

7

6. When pressing curved edges, clip sharp inward curves **(Diagram 23)**. If the shape doesn't curve smoothly, separate the paper from the fabric with your fingernail and try again.

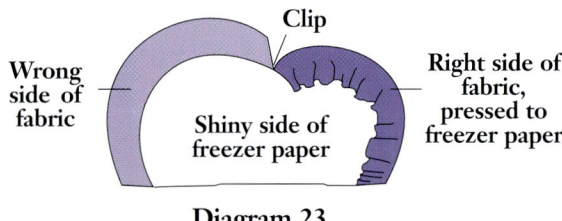

Diagram 23

Diagram 25

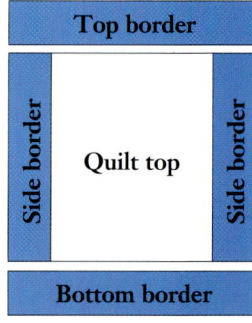

Diagram 26

7. Remove the pins when all seam allowances have been pressed to the freezer paper. Position the prepared appliqué right side up on the background fabric. Press to adhere it to the background fabric.

Machine Appliqué

A machine-sewn satin stitch makes a neat edging. For machine appliqué, cut appliqué pieces without adding seam allowances.

Using fusible web to adhere pieces to the background adds a stiff extra layer to the appliqué and is not appropriate for some quilts. It is best used on small pieces, difficult fabrics, or for wall hangings and accessories in which added stiffness is acceptable. The web prevents fraying and shifting during appliqué.

Place tear-away stabilizer under the background fabric behind the appliqué. Machine-stitch the appliqué edges with a satin stitch or close-spaced zigzag **(Diagram 24)**. Test the stitch length and width on a sample first. Use an open-toed presser foot. Remove the stabilizer when appliqué is complete.

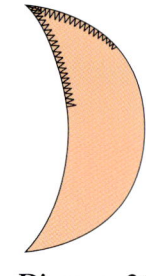

Diagram 24

Measuring Borders

Because seams may vary and fabrics may stretch a bit, opposite sides of your assembled quilt top may not be the same measurement. You can (and should) correct this when you add borders.

Measure the length of each side of the quilt. Trim the side border strips to match the *shorter* of the two sides. Join borders to the quilt as described below, easing the longer side of the quilt to fit the border. Join borders to the top and bottom edges in the same manner.

Straight Borders

Side borders are usually added first **(Diagram 25)**. With right sides facing and raw edges aligned, pin the center of one border strip to the center of one side of the quilt top. Pin the border to the quilt at each end and then pin along the side as desired. Machine-stitch with the border strip on top. Press the seam allowance toward the border. Trim excess border fabric at each end. In the same manner, add the border to the opposite side and then the top and bottom borders **(Diagram 26)**.

Mitered Borders

1. Measure your quilt sides. Trim the side border strips to fit the shorter side *plus* the width of the border *plus* 2".
2. Center the measurement of the shorter side on one border strip, placing a pin at each end and at the center of the measurement.
3. With right sides facing and raw edges aligned, match the pins on the border strip to the center and corners of the longer side of the quilt. (Border fabric will extend beyond the corners.)
4. Start machine-stitching at the top pin, backstitching to lock the stitches. Continue to sew, easing the quilt between pins. Stop at the last pin and backstitch. Join remaining borders in the same manner. Press seam allowances toward borders.
5. With right sides facing, fold the quilt diagonally, aligning the raw edges of adjacent borders. Pin securely **(Diagram 27)**.

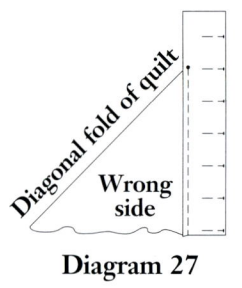

Diagram 27

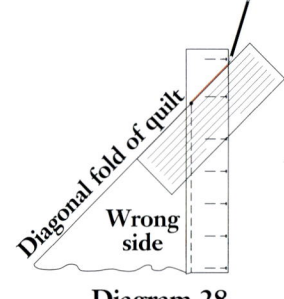

Diagram 28

6. Align a yardstick or quilter's ruler along the diagonal fold **(Diagram 28)**. Holding the ruler firmly, mark a line from the end of the border seam to the raw edge.
7. Start machine-stitching at the beginning of the marked line, backstitch, and then stitch on the line out to the raw edge.

8. Unfold the quilt to be sure that the corner lies flat. Correct the stitching if necessary. Trim the seam allowance to ¼".

9. Miter the remaining corners in the same manner. Press the corner seams open.

Quilting Without Marking

Some quilts can be quilted in-the-ditch (right along the seam line), outline-quilted (¼" from the seam line), or echo-quilted (lines of quilting rippling outward from the design like waves on a pond). These methods can be used without any marking at all. If you are machine quilting, simply use the edge of your presser foot and the seam line as a guide. If you are hand quilting, by the time you have pieced a quilt top, your eye will be practiced enough for you to produce straight, even quilting without the guidance of marked lines.

Marking Quilting Designs

Many quilters like to mark the entire top at one time, a practice that requires long-lasting markings. The most common tool for this purpose is a sharp **pencil**. However, most pencils are made with an oil-based graphite lead, which often will not wash out completely. Look for a high-quality artist's pencil marked "2H" or higher (the higher the number, the harder the lead, and the lighter the line it will make). Sharpen the pencil frequently to keep the line on the fabric thin and light. Or try a mechanical pencil with a 0.5-mm lead. It will maintain a fine line without sharpening.

While you are in the art supply store, get a **white plastic eraser** (brand name Magic Rub). This eraser, used by professional drafters and artists, will cleanly remove the carbon smudges left by pencil lead without fraying the fabric or leaving eraser crumbs.

Water- and **air-soluble marking pens** are convenient, but controversial, marking tools. Some quilters have found that the marks reappear, often up to several years later, while others have no problems with them.

Be sure to test these pens on each fabric you plan to mark and *follow package directions exactly*. Because the inks can be permanently set by heat, be very careful with a marked quilt. Do not leave it in your car on a hot day and never touch it with an iron until the marks have been removed. Plan to complete the quilting within a year after marking it with a water-soluble pen.

Air-soluble pens are best for marking small sections at a time. The marks disappear within 24 to 48 hours, but the ink remains in the fabric until it is washed. After the quilt is completed and before it is used, rinse it twice in clear, cool water, using no soap, detergent, or bleach. Let the quilt air-dry.

For dark fabrics, the cleanest marker you can use is a thin sliver of pure, white **soap**. Choose a soap that contains no creams, deodorants, dyes, or perfumes; these added ingredients may leave a residue on the fabric.

Other marking tools include **colored pencils** made specifically for marking fabric and **tailor's chalk** (available in powdered, stick, and traditional cake form). When using chalk, mark small sections of the quilt at a time because the chalk rubs off easily.

Quilting Stencils

Quilting patterns can be purchased as precut stencils. Simply lay these on your quilt top and mark the design through the cutout areas.

To make your own stencil of a printed quilting pattern, such as the one below, use a permanent marker to trace the design onto a blank sheet of template plastic. Then use a craft knife to cut out the design.

Quilting Stencil Pattern

Making a Quilt Backing

Some fabric and quilt shops sell 90" and 108" widths of 100% cotton fabric that are very practical for quilt backing. However, the instructions in this book always give backing yardage based on 44"-wide fabric.

When using 44"-wide fabric, all quilts wider than 41" will require a pieced backing. For quilts 41" to 80" wide, you will need an amount of fabric equal to two times the desired *length* of the unfinished backing. (The unfinished backing should be at least 3" larger on all sides than the quilt top.)

The simplest method of making a backing is to cut the fabric in half widthwise **(Diagram 29)**, and then sew the two panels together lengthwise. This results in a backing with a vertical center seam. Press the seam allowances to one side.

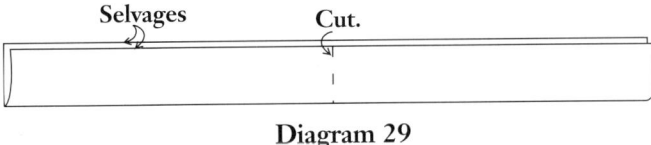

Diagram 29

Another method of seaming the backing results in two vertical seams and a center panel of fabric. This method is often preferred by quilt show judges. Begin by cutting the fabric in half widthwise. Open the two lengths and stack them, with right sides facing and selvages aligned. Stitch along *both* selvage edges to create a tube of fabric **(Diagram 30)**. Cut down the center of the top layer of fabric only and open the fabric flat **(Diagram 31)**. Press seam allowances to one side.

If the quilt is wider than 80", it is more economical to cut the fabric into three lengths that are the desired width of the backing. Join the three lengths so that the seams are horizontal to the quilt, rather than vertical. For this method, you'll need an amount of fabric equal to three times the *width* of the unfinished backing.

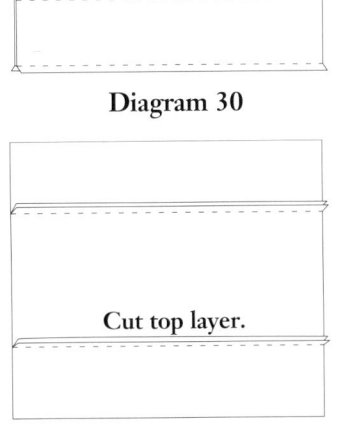

Diagram 30

Diagram 31

Fabric requirements in this book reflect the most economical method of seaming the backing fabric.

Layering and Basting

After the quilt top and backing are made, the next steps are layering and basting in preparation for quilting.

Prepare a large working surface to spread out the quilt—a large table, two tables pushed together, or the floor. Place the backing on the working surface wrong side up. Unfold the batting and place it on top of the backing, smoothing away any wrinkles or lumps.

Lay the quilt top wrong side down on top of the batting and backing. Make sure the edges of the backing and quilt top are parallel.

Knot a long strand of sewing thread and use a long (darning) needle for basting. Begin basting in the center of the quilt and baste out toward the edges. The basting stitches should cover an ample amount of the quilt so that the layers do not shift during quilting.

Machine quilters use nickel-plated safety pins for basting so there will be no basting threads to get caught on the presser foot. Safety pins, spaced approximately 4" apart, can be used by hand quilters, too.

Hand Quilting

Hand-quilted stitches should be evenly spaced, with the spaces between stitches about the same length as the stitches themselves. The *number* of stitches per inch is less important than the *uniformity* of the stitching. Don't worry if you take only five or six stitches per inch; just be consistent throughout the project.

Machine Quilting

For machine quilting, the backing and batting should be 3" larger all around than the quilt top, because the quilting process pushes the quilt top fabric outward. After quilting, trim the backing and batting to the same size as the quilt top.

Thread your bobbin with good-quality sewing thread (not quilting thread) in a color to match the backing. Use a top thread color to match the quilt top or use invisible nylon thread.

An even-feed or walking foot will feed all the quilt's layers through the machine at the same speed. It is possible to machine-quilt without this foot (by experimenting with tension and presser foot pressure), but it will be much easier *with* it. If you do not have this foot, get one from your sewing machine dealer.

Straight-Grain Binding

1. Mark the fabric in horizontal lines the width of the binding **(Diagram 32)**.

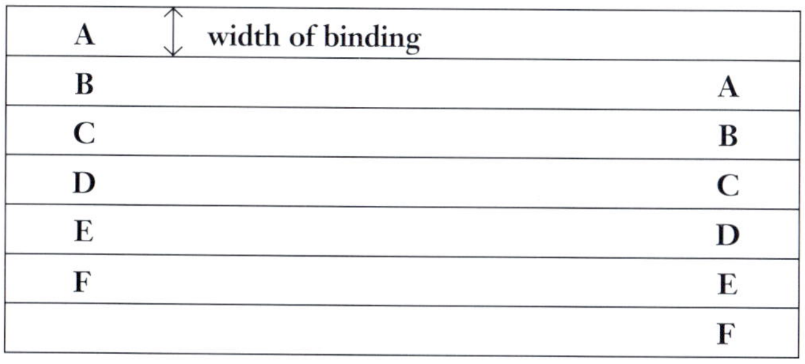

A	width of binding	
B		A
C		B
D		C
E		D
F		E
		F

Diagram 32

2. With right sides facing, fold the fabric in half, offsetting drawn lines by matching letters and raw edges **(Diagram 33)**. Stitch a ¼" seam.
3. Cut the binding in a continuous strip, starting with one end and following the marked lines around the tube. Press the strip in half lengthwise.

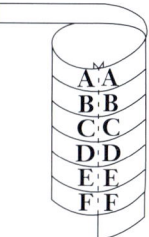

Diagram 33

Continuous Bias Binding

This technique can be used to make continuous bias for appliqué as well as for binding.

1. Cut a square of fabric in half diagonally to form two triangles. With right sides facing, join the triangles **(Diagram 34)**. Press the seam allowance open.

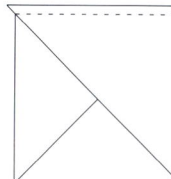

Diagram 34

2. Mark parallel lines the desired width of the binding **(Diagram 35)**, taking care not to stretch the bias. With right sides facing, align the raw edges (indicated as Seam 2). As you align the edges, offset one Seam 2 point past its natural matching point by one line. Stitch the seam; then press the seam allowance open.

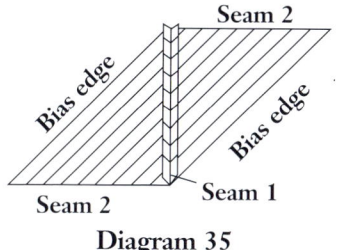

Diagram 35

3. Cut the binding in a continuous strip, starting with the protruding point and following the marked lines around the tube **(Diagram 36)**. Press the strip in half lengthwise.

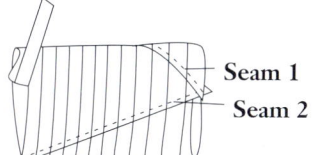

Diagram 36

Applying Binding

Binding is applied to the front of the quilt first. You may begin anywhere on the edge of the quilt except at the corner.

1. Matching raw edges, lay the binding on the quilt. Fold down the top corner of the binding at a 45° angle, align the raw edges, and pin **(Diagram 37)**.

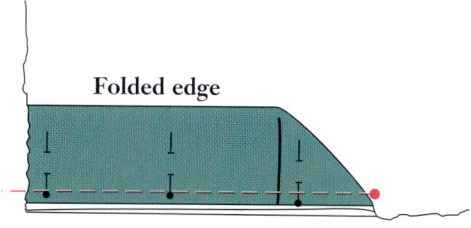

Diagram 37

2. Beginning at the folded end, machine-stitch the binding to the quilt. Stop stitching ¼" from the corner and backstitch. Fold the binding strip diagonally away from the quilt, making a 45° angle **(Diagram 38)**.
3. Fold the binding strip straight down along the next side to be stitched, creating a pleat in the corner. Position the needle at the ¼" seam line of the new side **(Diagram 39)**. Make a few stitches, backstitch, and then stitch the seam. Continue until all corners and sides are done. Overlap the end of the binding strip over the beginning fold and stitch about 2" beyond it. Trim any excess binding.

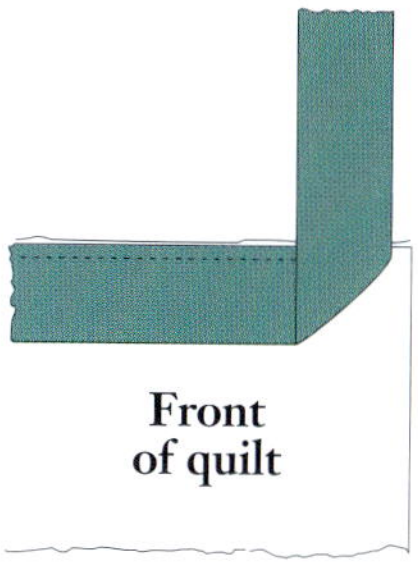

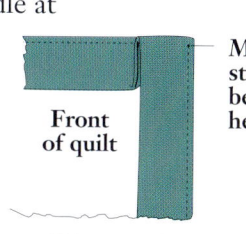

Diagram 38

Diagram 39

4. Turn the binding over the raw edge of the quilt. Slipstitch it in place on the back, using thread that matches the binding. The fold at the beginning of the binding strip will create a neat, angled edge when it is folded to the back.
5. At each corner, fold the binding to form a miter **(Diagram 40)**. Hand-stitch the miters closed if desired.

Diagram 40

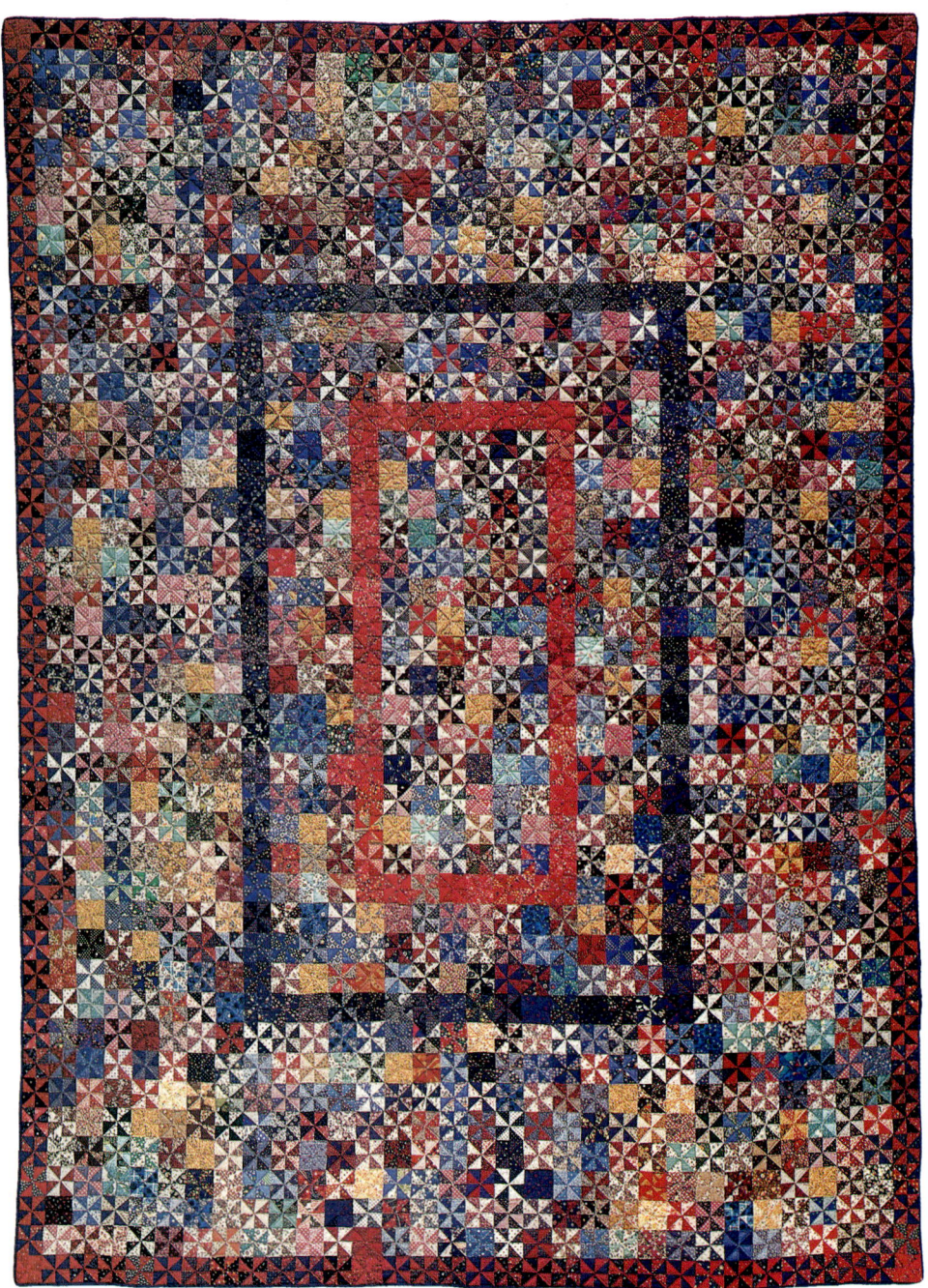

Quilt by Jean Briggs
Gambier, Ohio

Pinwheel

Jean Briggs's quilt offers you a chance to exhaust your scrap pile. Jean took the design from an antique quilt she spied at a quilt show. To give the set some focus, she placed a rectangle of blue print blocks outside a rectangle of red print blocks. Jean pieced this one entirely by hand, but you may choose machine piecing if you prefer.

Finished Quilt Size
80" x 107½"

Number of Blocks and Finished Size
1,376 blocks   2½" x 2½"

Fabric Requirements
Red prints   1⅞ yards
Blue prints   2¼ yards
Dark prints   7¼ yards*
Light/medium prints   7¼ yards*
Blue for binding   1¼ yards
Backing   6¼ yards

*You may select red and blue prints also. The fabric requirements for red and blue prints above are for the Pinwheel blocks in the red and blue rectangles and borders. See Step 1.

Number to Cut**
Square
   template   484 red prints
                 596 blue prints
                 2,212 dark prints
                 2,212 light/medium prints

**Fabric squares are cut diagonally into 2 triangles. See Step 1.

Quilt Top Assembly

1. Group 2 squares from 1 blue print and 2 squares from 1 red print into a set of 4. Group 142 sets. Group squares from 2 different blue prints into 78 sets of 4. Group 50 sets using 2 different red prints. Group remaining squares using 1 dark print and 1 light/medium print into 1,106 sets of 4.

2. Cut each square in half diagonally to make 2 triangles. (Keep triangles grouped in sets.)

With right sides facing and raw edges aligned, join contrasting triangles from each set to form triangle-squares, as shown in **Block Assembly Diagram**. Join triangle-squares to complete 1 Pinwheel block. Repeat for each set to make a total of 1,376 blocks.

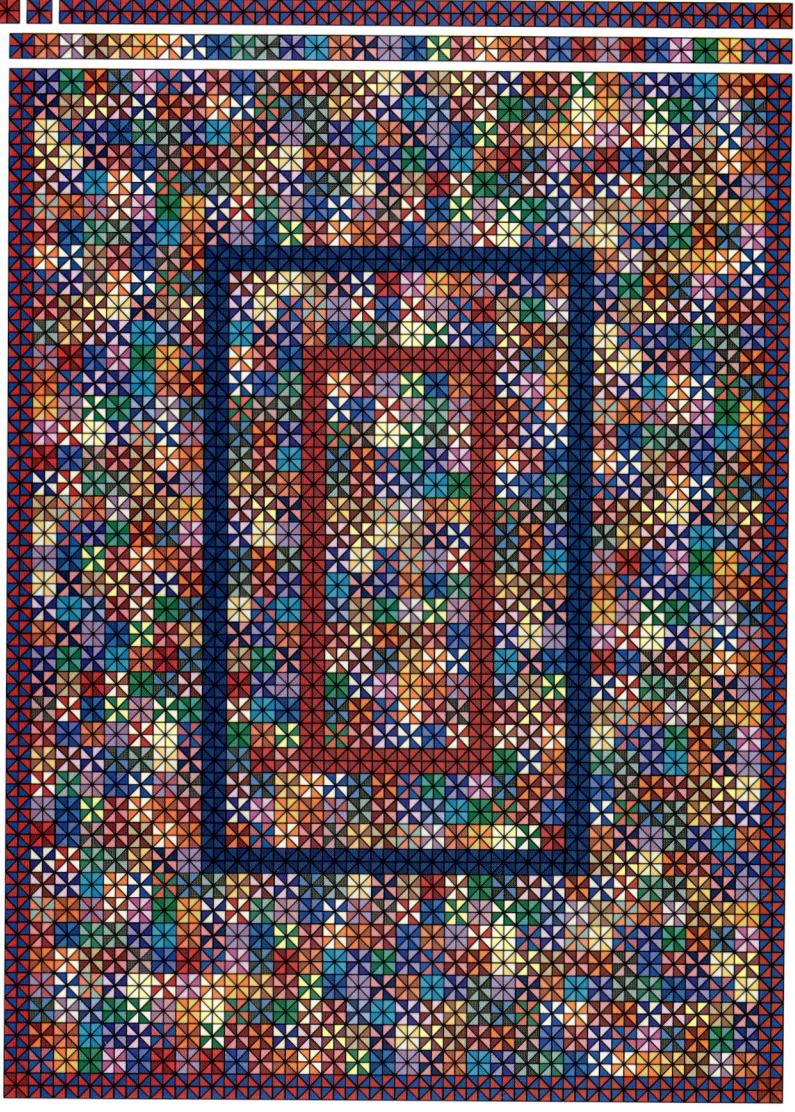

Setting Diagram

3. Referring to **Setting Diagram**, arrange blocks in 43 rows of 32 blocks each. Join rows. Note placement of blue print and red print Pinwheel blocks on outside edges and red print Pinwheel blocks on quilt corners.

Quilting
Outline-quilt outside seam lines of alternate triangles.

Finished Edges
Referring to instructions on page 11, make 10½ yards of 2"-wide bias or straight-grain binding from blue. Apply binding to quilt edges.

Triangle Square

Block Assembly Diagram

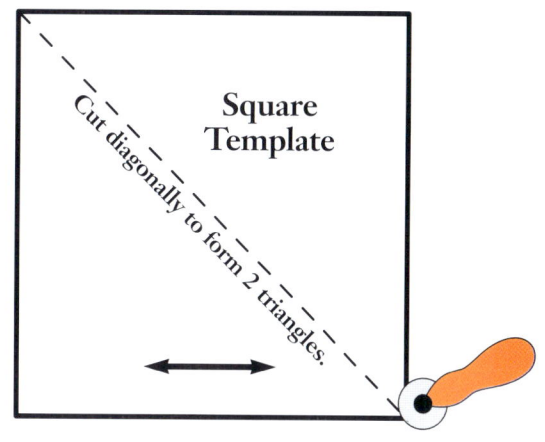

Square Template

Cut diagonally to form 2 triangles.

*Quilt by Pepper Cory
Lansing, Michigan*

Flying Under Radar

Pepper Cory pieced the majority of *Flying Under Radar*, a Drunkard's Path variation, during the winter of 1990–1991. Like most of America, Pepper says, "I was engrossed by the Gulf War. The Stealth airplanes somehow related to the winged images emerging from the quilt and I was reminded of my father, a World War II pilot, and his experiences flying 'under radar' in northern Italy. This quilt has evolved into a memorial quilt to my father and to all other pilots, known and unknown, who flew under radar."

Finished Quilt Size
88" x 88"

Number of Blocks and Finished Size
216 Drunkard's Path blocks — 4" x 4"
108 Four-Patch blocks — 4" x 4"

Fabric Requirements
Off-white — 2¼ yards
Assorted light prints — 3 yards
Assorted dark prints — 3 yards
Backing — 8 yards
Red for binding — 1 yard

Number to Cut
Template A — 216 dark prints
Template B — 216 light prints
Template C — 216 light prints
          — 216 dark prints
Template D — 84 dark prints

Quilt Top Assembly
1. From off-white, cut 2 (4½" x 72½") and 2 (4½" x 80½") border strips.

2. Referring to **Drunkard's Path Block Assembly Diagram**, join 1 dark print A and 1 light print B to make 1 Drunkard's Path block. (Refer to page 6, Step 9 for more information on piecing curves.) Repeat to make 216 Drunkard's Path blocks.
Referring to **Four-Patch Block Assembly Diagram**, join 2 light print Cs and 2 dark print Cs to make 1 Four-Patch block. Repeat to make 108 Four-Patch blocks.

3. For each row, refer to **Setting Diagram** for color placement and join 12 Drunkard's Path blocks and 6 Four-Patch blocks as shown. Make 18 rows. Join rows.

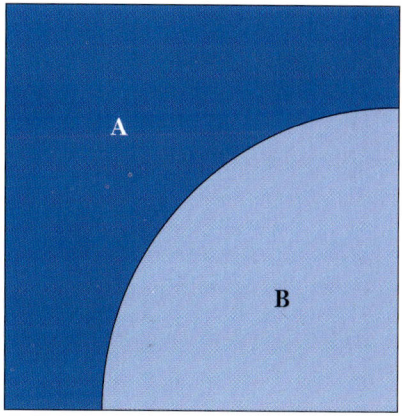

Drunkard's Path Assembly Diagram

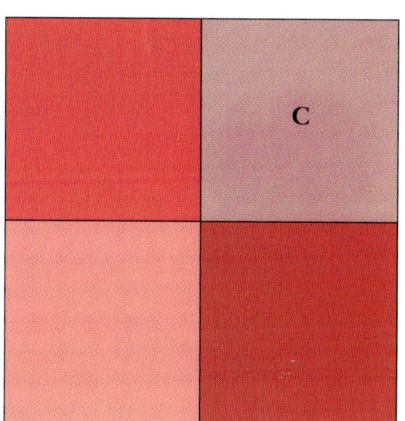

Four-Patch Assembly Diagram

4. Join 4½" x 72½" off-white border strips to top and bottom edges of quilt. Join 4½" x 80½" off-white border strips to sides of quilt, butting corners.

5. To make top pieced border, join 20 dark print Ds as shown in **Setting Diagram**. Repeat to make bottom border. Join borders to top and bottom edges of quilt. To make 1 side pieced border, join 22 Ds. Repeat to make second side pieced border. Join borders to sides of quilt, butting corners.

Quilting
Quilt As, Bs, Cs, and Ds in-the-ditch or ¼" inside seam line, or quilt as desired. Quilt border as desired.

Finished Edges
Referring to instructions on page 11, make 10 yards of 2"-wide bias or straight-grain binding from red. Apply binding to quilt edges.

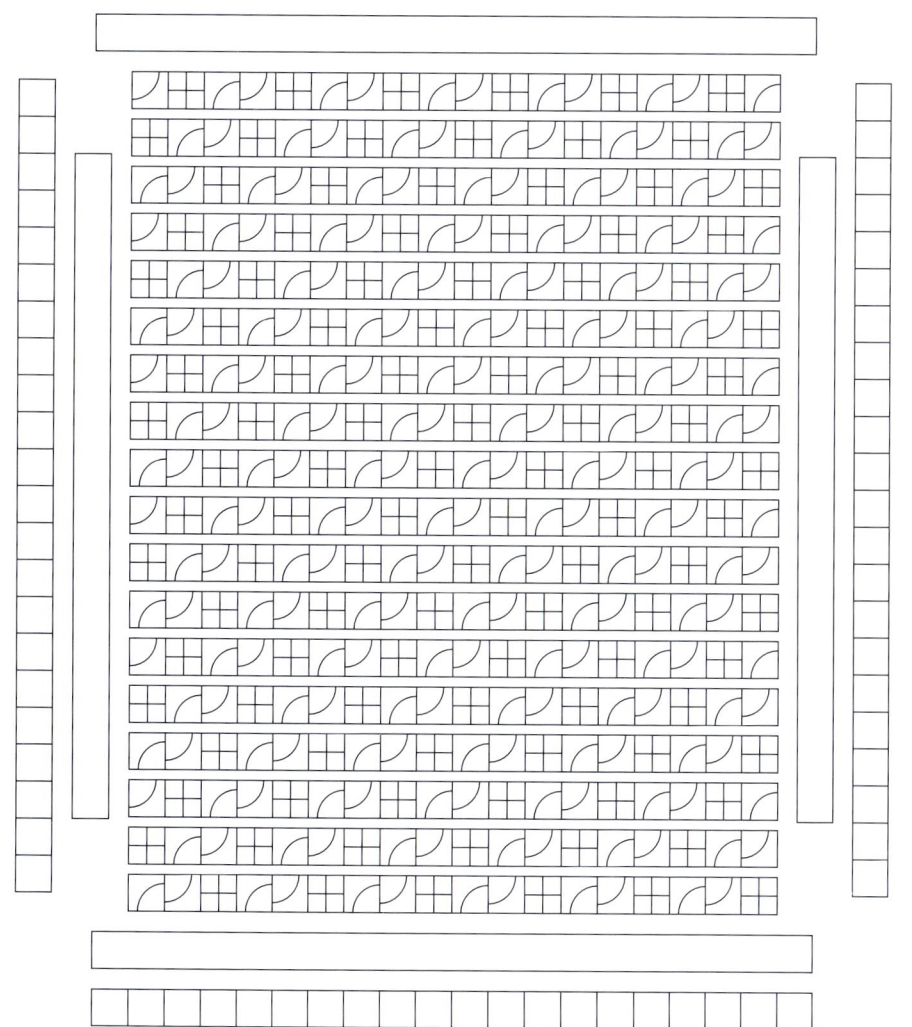

Setting Diagram

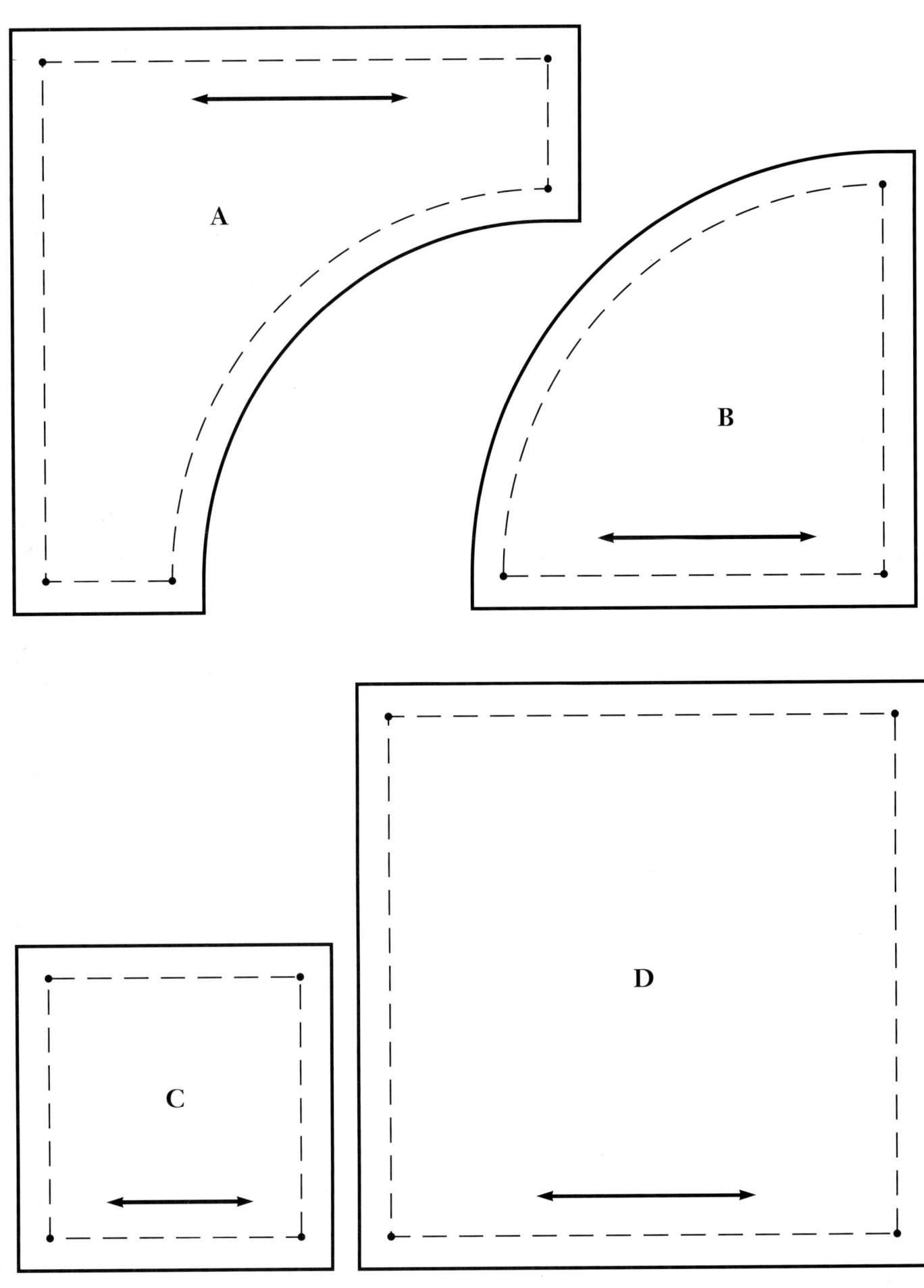

Quilt by Alvida Baltzell
Bristol, South Dakota

Windmills

This quilt belongs to Oxmoor House crafts editor Linda Wright. It was made by her grandmother, Alvida Baltzell, as a wedding gift for Linda and her husband, Kneeland, more than 20 years ago. Alvida chose to tie her quilt, and we've given you instructions for tying. However, feel free to hand- or machine quilt if you prefer.

Finished Quilt Sizes

Twin-size   63" x 88"
Full-size   75½" x 88"
Queen-size   88" x 100½"
King-size   100½" x 100½"

Fabric Requirements

Twin-size
   Red prints   1⅛ yards
   Red solids   2 yards
   Whites   2⅜ yards
   Backing   5½ yards

Full-size
   Red prints   1¼ yards
   Red solids   2½ yards
   Whites   2⅜ yards
   Backing   5½ yards

Queen-size
   Red prints   1⅝ yards
   Red solids   2¾ yards
   Whites   3 yards
   Backing   8 yards

King-size
   Red prints   1⅞ yards
   Red solids   3 yards
   Whites   3½ yards
   Backing   9½ yards

Other Materials

Pearl cotton

Number to Cut

Twin-size
   Triangle
   template   140 red print
              140 red solid
              280 white

Full-size
   Triangle
   template   168 red print
              168 red solid
              336 white

Queen-size
   Triangle
   template   224 red print
              224 red solid
              448 white

King-size
   Triangle
   template   256 red print
              256 red solid
              512 white

Quilt Top Assembly

1. For twin-size quilt, cut 30 (3½" x 9½") and 4 (3½" x 85") sashing strips from red solid.

For full-size quilt, cut 36 (3½" x 9½") and 5 (3½" x 85") sashing strips from red solid.

For queen-size quilt, cut 49 (3½" x 9½") and 6 (3½" x 97½") sashing strips from solid.

For king-size quilt, cut 56 (3½" x 9½") and 7 (3½" x 97½") sashing strips from solid.

2. Referrring to **Block Assembly Diagram**, make 35 blocks for twin-size, 42 blocks for full-size, 56 blocks for queen-size, and 64 blocks for king-size quilt.

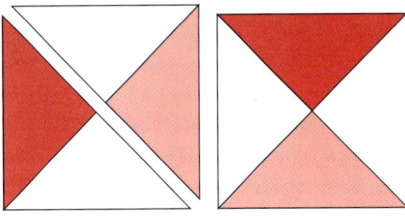
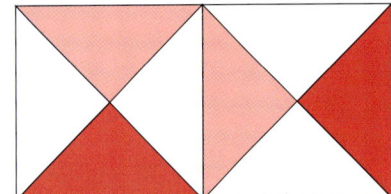

Block Assembly Diagram

3. Referring to **Setting Diagram** for desired quilt size, join blocks and sashing strips.

4. Prepare backing to extend 3" beyond edges of quilt top.

Tying

To tie quilt, cut pearl cotton into 16" lengths. Thread needle with doubled length of pearl cotton. Beginning at center of quilt, tie square knots at center and corners of each block.

If you don't wish to tie quilt, quilt blocks and sashing as desired.

Finished Edges

For self-binding, fold 2" of backing to front of quilt. Turn under ¼" seam allowance and slipstitch to quilt top, mitering corners.

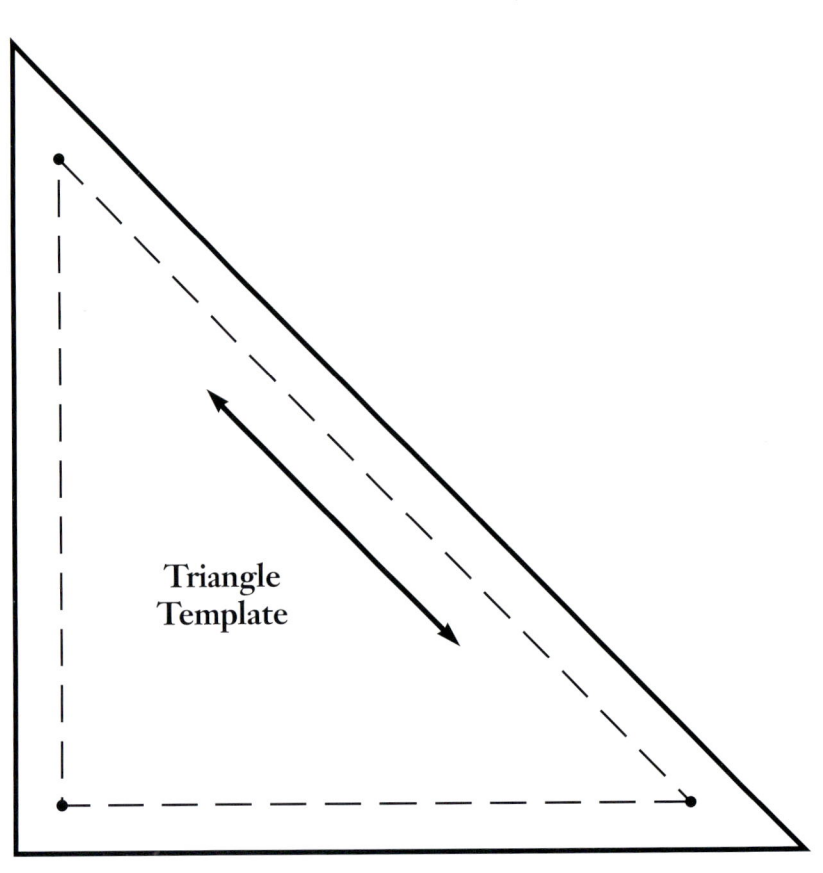

Triangle Template

Twin-size Setting Diagram

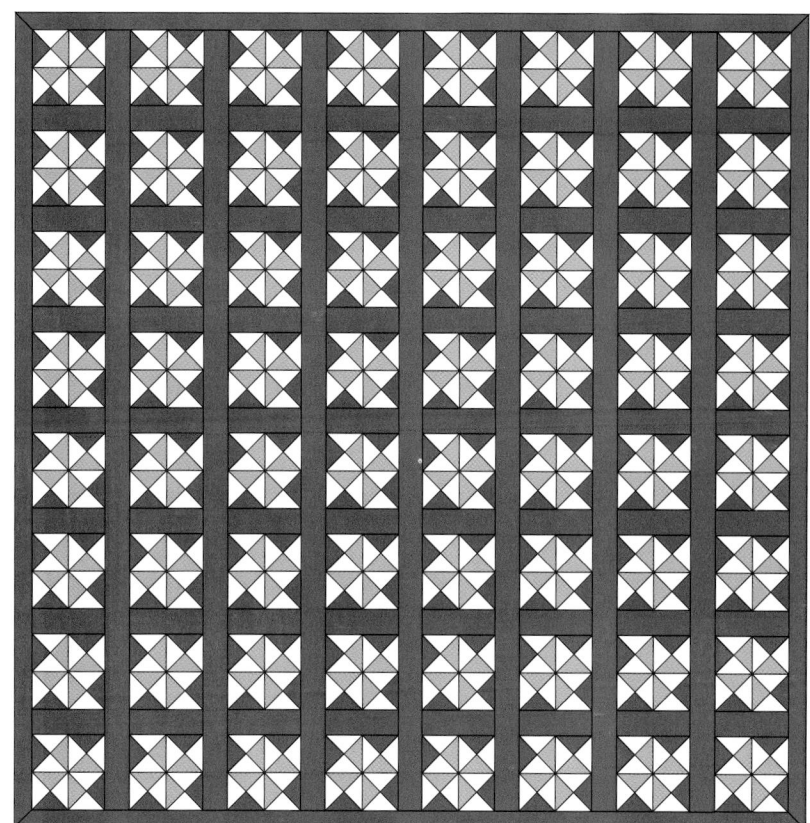

King-size Setting Diagram

Full-size Setting Diagram

Queen-size Setting Diagram

Quilt by Corrie B. Corkern
Franklinton, LA

Arkansas Crossroads

Looking for a pattern that would use some of her fabric scraps, Corrie Corkern found the Arkansas Crossroads block in a book of scrap quilt patterns and knew immediately that it was the one she wanted to make. Using as many different scraps as possible, Corrie finished the quilt during the summer of 1993. *Arkansas Crossroads* won a blue ribbon at the 1993 Washington Parish Fair.

Finished Quilt Size
80" x 96"

Number of Blocks and Finished Size
80 blocks   8" x 8"

Fabric Requirements
Red print   2½ yards
Yellow print   2⅜ yards
Assorted light prints   3 yards
Assorted medium prints   3 yards
Assorted dark prints   2 yards
Backing   5¾ yards
Red print for binding   1 yard

Number to Cut
Template A   320 light prints
                320 medium prints
                320 dark prints
Template B   320 light prints
                320 medium prints

Quilt Top Assembly

1. From yellow print, cut 2 (2½" x 70½") and 2 (2½" x 82½") inner border strips. From red print, cut 2 (6½" x 82½") and 2 (6½" x 86½") outer border strips. Set aside.

2. Referring to **Block Assembly Diagram**, join 4 light print As, 4 medium print As, 4 dark print As, 4 light print Bs, and 4 medium print Bs to make 1 block. Make 80 blocks.

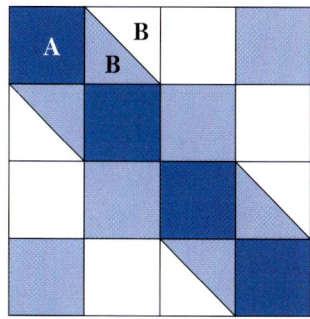

Block Assembly Diagram

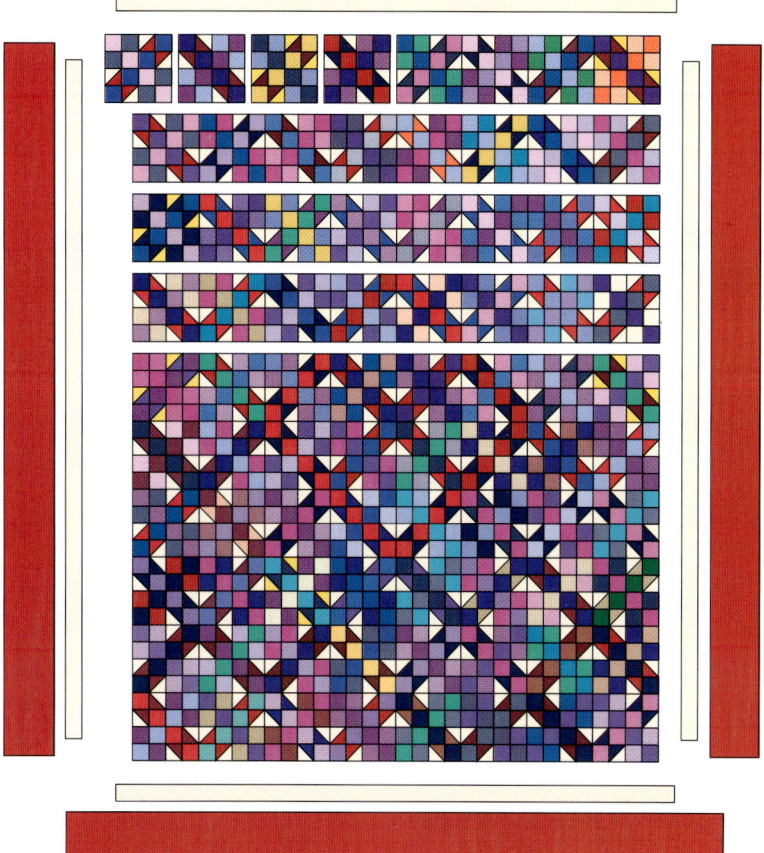

Setting Diagram

3. Refer to **Setting Diagram** and turn blocks to alternate direction of diagonal stripes as shown. Join 8 blocks to make 1 row. Repeat to make 10 rows. Join rows.

4. Join 2½" x 82½" yellow print borders to sides of quilt. Join 2½" x 70½" yellow print borders to top and bottom edges of quilt, butting corners.

   ?" x 86½" red print
des of quilt. Join
6½" x 82½" red print borders to top and bottom edges of quilt, butting corners.

Quilting
Quilt in-the-ditch around each star and around each group of 4 squares or quilt as desired.

Finished Edges
Referring to instructions on page 11, make 10 yards of 2"-wide bias or straight-grain binding from red print. Apply binding to quilt edges.

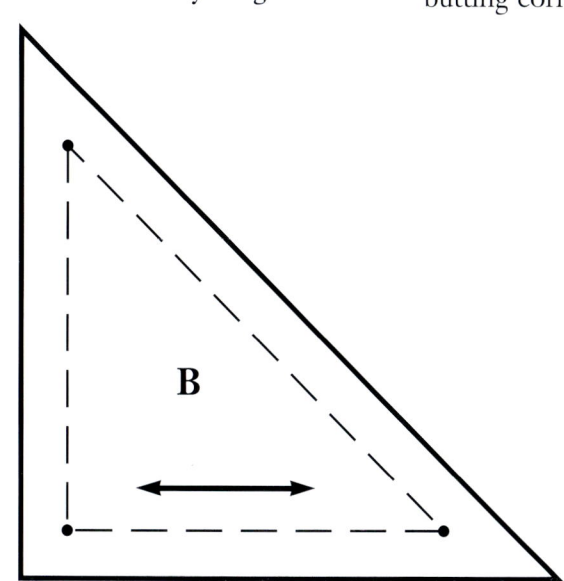

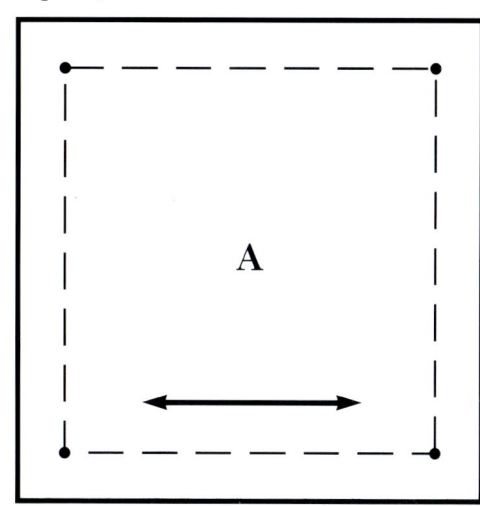

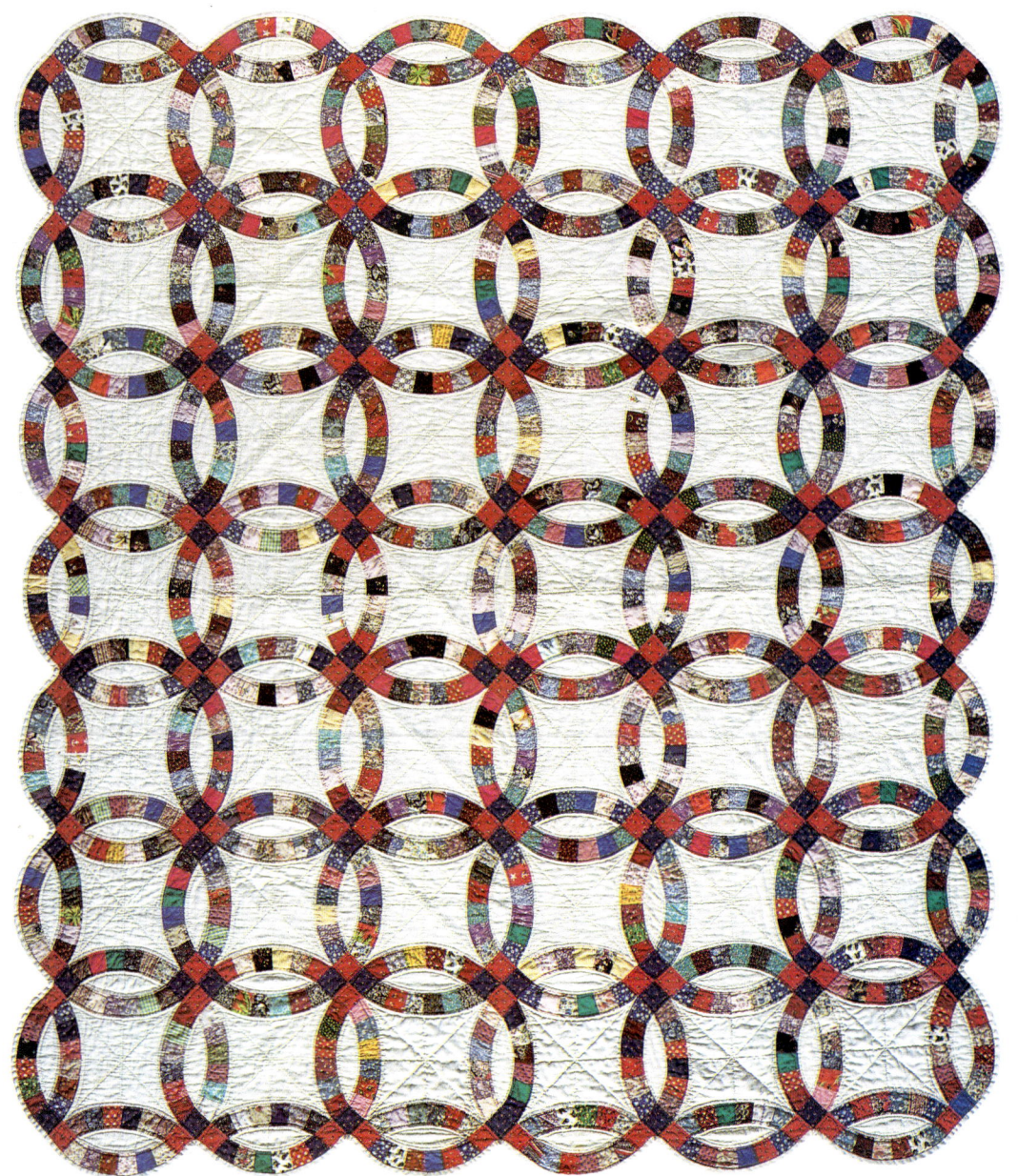

*Quilt by Mary E. Ramey
Leeds, Alabama*

Double Wedding Ring

Many quilt historians believe this beautiful pattern came into being in the mid- to late-19th century. Whatever its origin, there's no doubt that *Double Wedding Ring* is one of the most cherished of all quilts. In fact, it may well be the most often-pieced pattern in the whole collection of American quilts.

In addition to template patterns for a full-size quilt, we have given you patterns for a smaller version, which makes a lovely wall hanging or crib quilt. (For a king-size quilt, use the full-size templates and add 2 rows of rings to 1 side and 2 rows to the bottom of the full-size layout.)

Finished Sizes
Full-size   71⅝" x 72¾"
Crib   27⅛" x 31½"

Fabric Requirements
Full-size
    Assorted scraps   5 yards
    White   4¼ yards
    Backing   5 yards
    Bias binding   1 yard

Crib
    Assorted scraps   2 yards
    White   1¾ yards
    Backing   1 yard
    Bias binding   ¾ yard

Number to Cut
Template A	194 assorted
Template A rev.	194 assorted
Template B	776 assorted
Template C	194 assorted
Template D	97 white
Template E	42 white

Quilt Top Assembly
1. Referring to **Ring Assembly Diagram,** make 21 rings. Follow **Setting Diagram** to make partial rings.

Note: You will have 10 Es remaining after making whole rings and partial rings.

2. Referring to **Setting Diagram,** join whole rings, partial rings, and remaining Es.

Quilting
Quilt as desired.

Finished Edges
Referring to instructions on page 11, make 2"-wide bias binding. Apply binding to quilt edges.

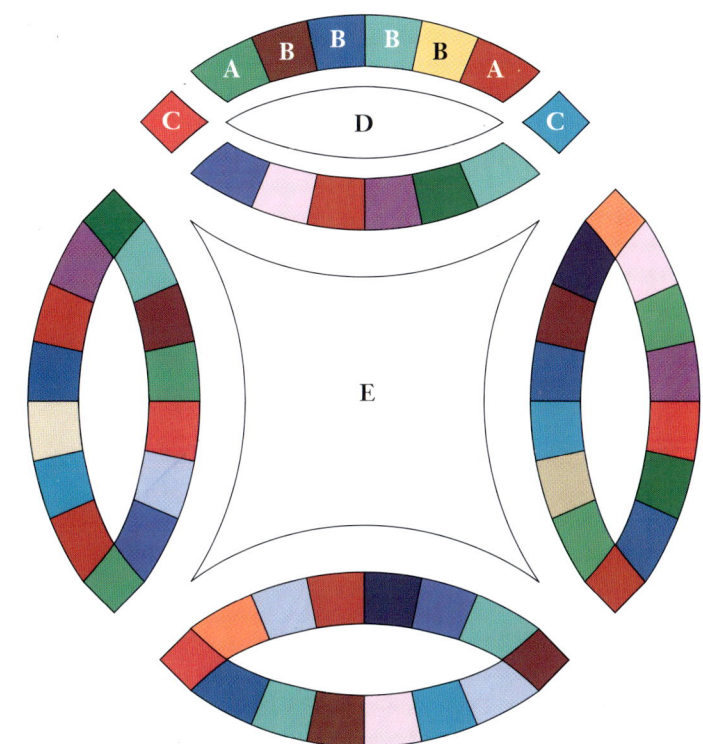

Ring Assembly Diagram

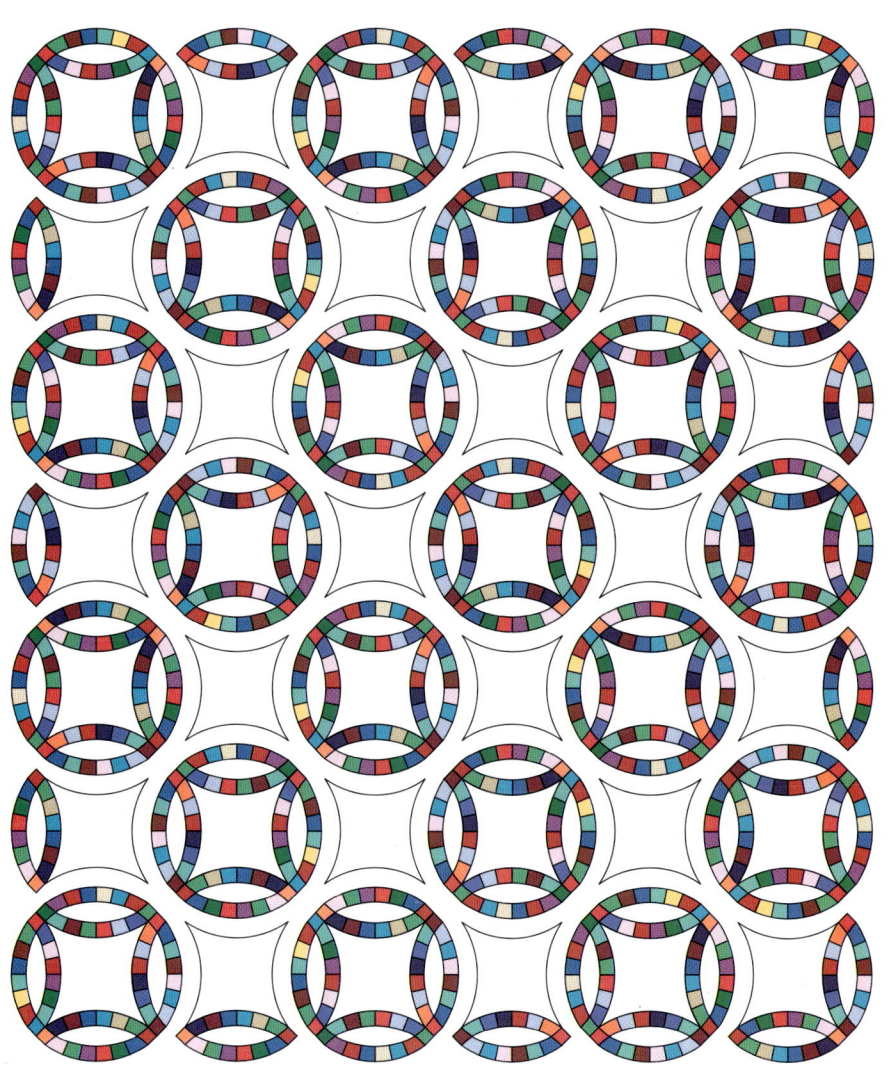

Setting Diagram

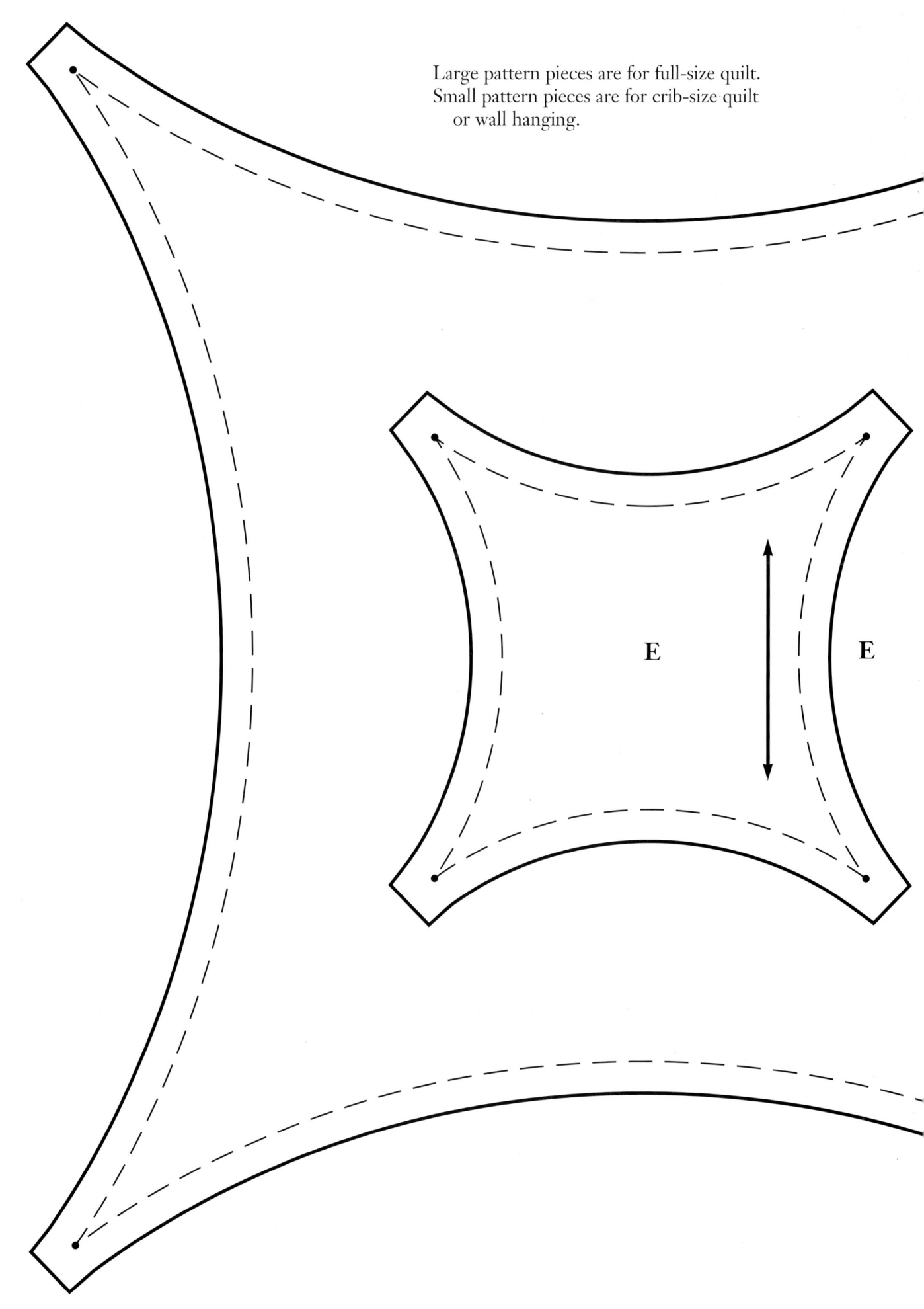

Large pattern pieces are for full-size quilt. Small pattern pieces are for crib-size quilt or wall hanging.

E

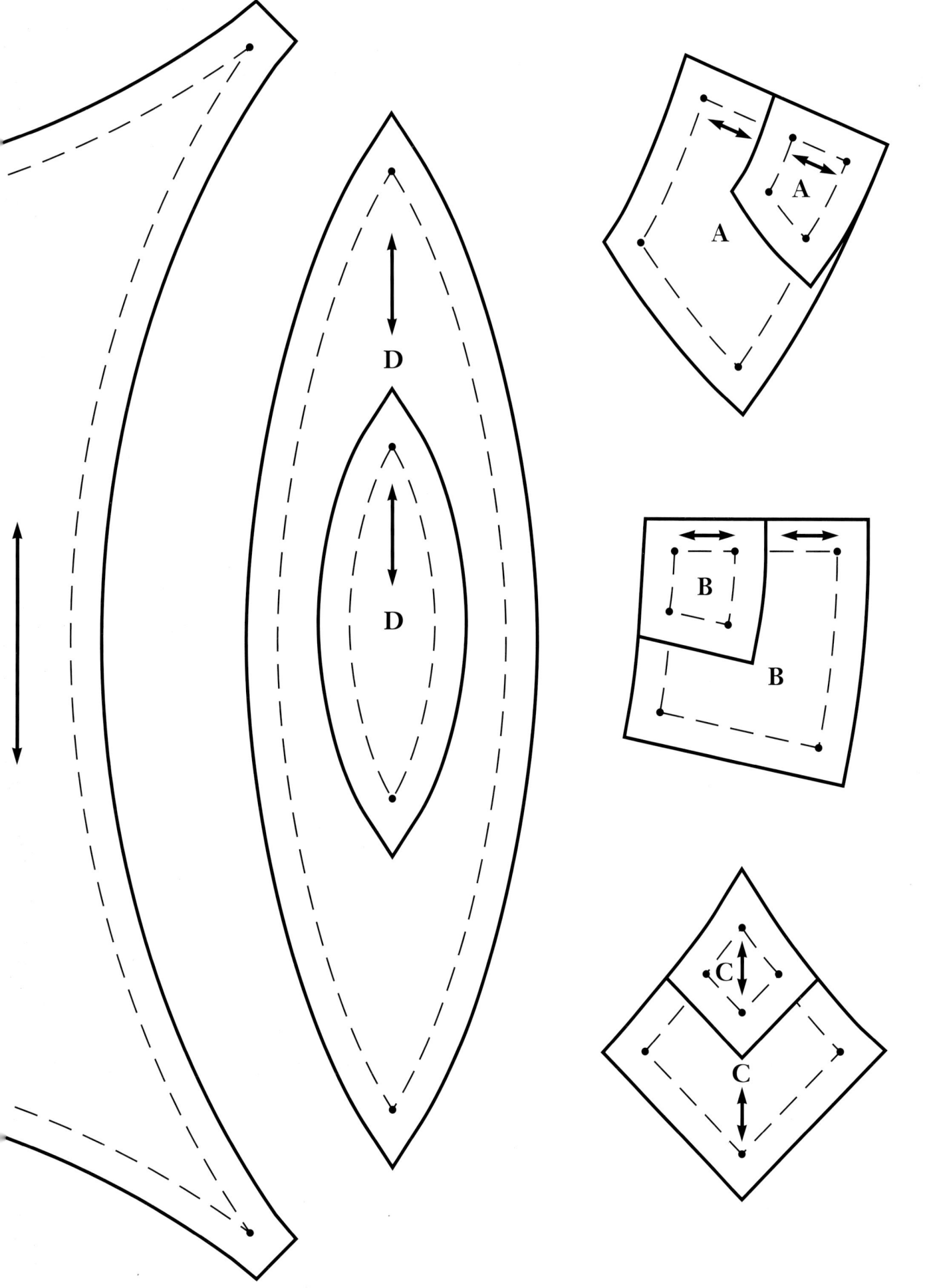

Quilt by Mary Ann Keathley
Jacksonville, Arkansas

3-D Nine-Patch

Mary Ann Keathley had been looking for an unusual setting for her Nine-Patch blocks when she saw a streak-of-lightning design that appealed to her. So she took that design and added a twist to it. "Instead of using one color, I decided to use both light and dark fabrics. This gives the quilt the three-dimensional effect," Mary Ann says. Sometimes all it takes is a slight variation on a well-known theme to create a new and stunning look!

Finished Quilt Size
82½" x 97½"

Number of Blocks and Finished Size
86 blocks   6" x 6"

Fabric Requirements
Scraps   2¾ yards
Muslin   3½ yards
Green   2¾ yards
Dark green print   3½ yards*
Backing   5½ yards

*Includes fabric for binding.

Number To Cut
Template A   26 muslin
Template B   100 green
              100 dark green print
Template C   4 muslin

Quilt Top Assembly

1. From green, cut 2 (1¾" x 75") border strips, 2 (1¾" x 83") strips, 2 (1¾" x 90") strips, and 2 (1¾" x 98") strips. Set aside.

Cut all scraps in 2½"-wide strips. From strips, cut 26 (2½") squares. Set aside.

Cut remaining muslin in 2½"-wide crosswise strips.

2. To make Panel 1, join 2 scrap strips and 1 muslin strip as shown in **Panel Diagram**. Repeat to make 11 Panel 1s.

To make Panel 2, join 1 scrap strip and 2 muslin strips as shown in **Panel Diagram**. Repeat to make 14 Panel 2s.

Cut each pieced panel crosswise into 2½" strips.

3. Referring to **Block Assembly Diagram**, join 2 Panel 1s and 1 Panel 2 to make 1 Nine-Patch block. Repeat to make 86 Nine-Patch blocks. Set aside remaining pieced Panel 2s for borders.

4. Referring to **Block Assembly Diagram**, join parallelograms (B) to sides of 50 Nine-Patch blocks to make 3-D Nine-Patch blocks. Join 3-D Nine-Patch blocks in 5 vertical rows of 10 blocks each as shown in **Row Assembly Diagram**.

5. On large working surface, arrange 3-D Nine-Patch blocks, remaining Nine-Patch blocks, and

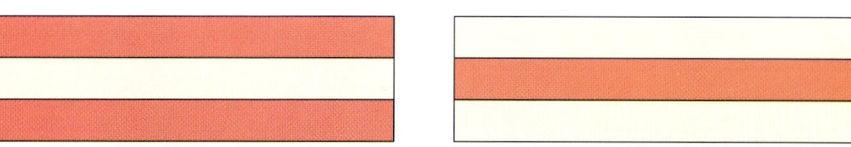

Panel 1—Make 11.   Panel 2—Make 14.

Panel Diagram

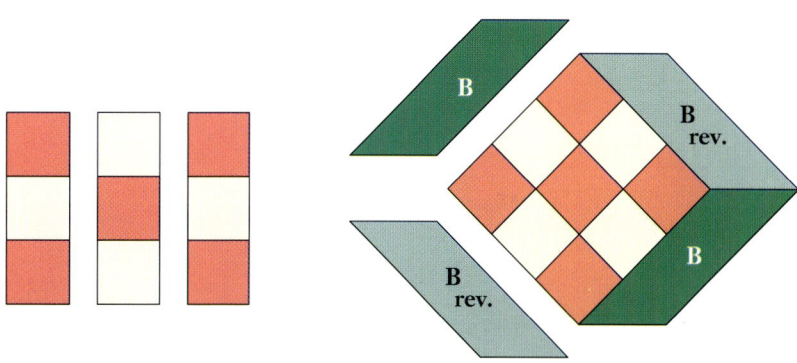

Figure 1   Figure 2

Block Assembly Diagram

Row Assembly Diagram

triangles (A) in vertical rows, referring to **Setting Diagram**. Place 1 (2½") scrap square (cut in Step 1) in corner of 1 A, aligning raw edges. Appliqué inner edges of square (those not aligned with raw edges of A) to A. Repeat to applique remaining scrap squares to remaining As.

6. Referring to photograph and **Setting Diagram**, join rows of 3-D Nine-Patch blocks, Nine-Patch blocks, and As. Join corner triangles (C).

7. Join 1¾" x 75" border strips to top and bottom edges of quilt. Join 1¾" x 90" border strips to sides of quilt, mitering corners.

8. To make top diamond border, join 27 pieced Panel 2s as shown in **Border Assembly Diagram**. Trim points of muslin squares as shown. Repeat to make bottom diamond border. Join diamond borders to top and bottom edges of quilt.

To make 1 side diamond border, join 32 pieced Panel 2s. Trim points of muslin squares as shown. Repeat to make second side diamond border. Join to sides of quilt.

9. Join 1¾" x 83" border strips to top and bottom edges of quilt. Join 1¾" x 98" border strips to sides of quilt, mitering corners.

Quilting

Outline-quilt all blocks, border squares, and borders. Quilt along the diagonal of each muslin square.

Finished Edges

Referring to instructions on page 11, make 10½ yards of 2"-wide bias or straight-grain binding from dark green. Apply binding to quilt edges.

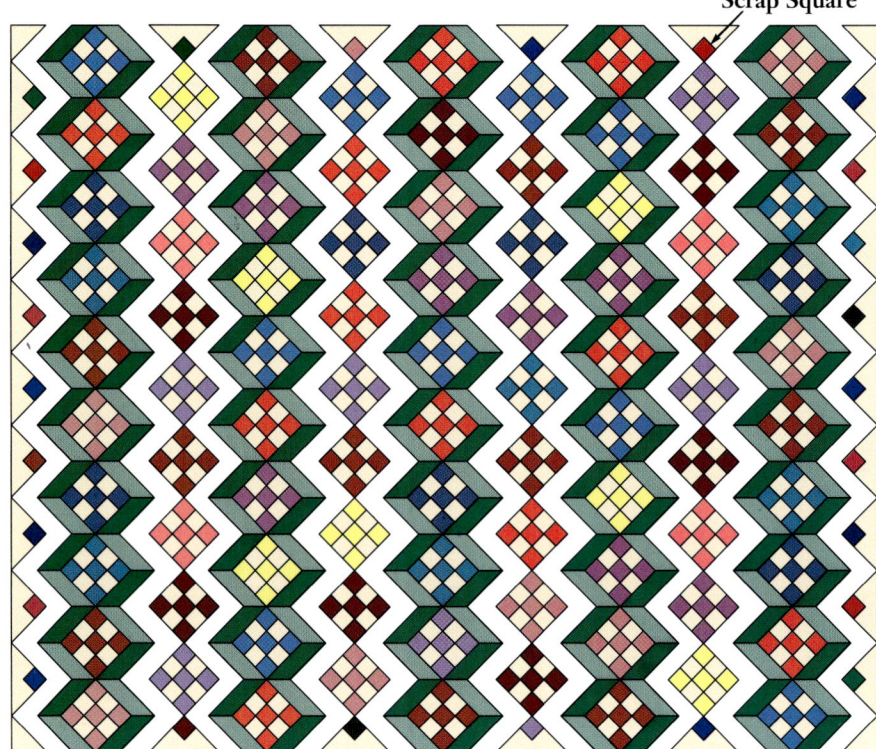

Setting Diagram

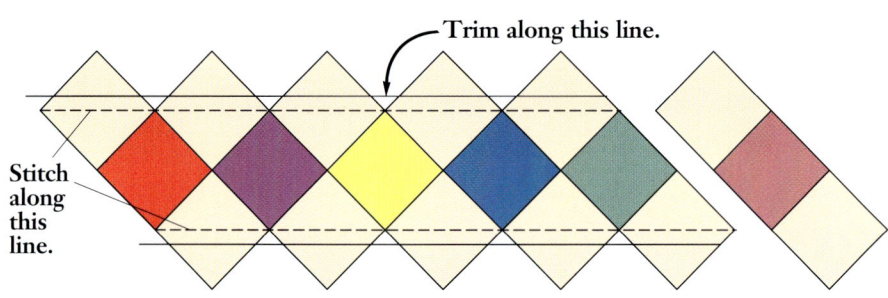

Border Assembly Diagram

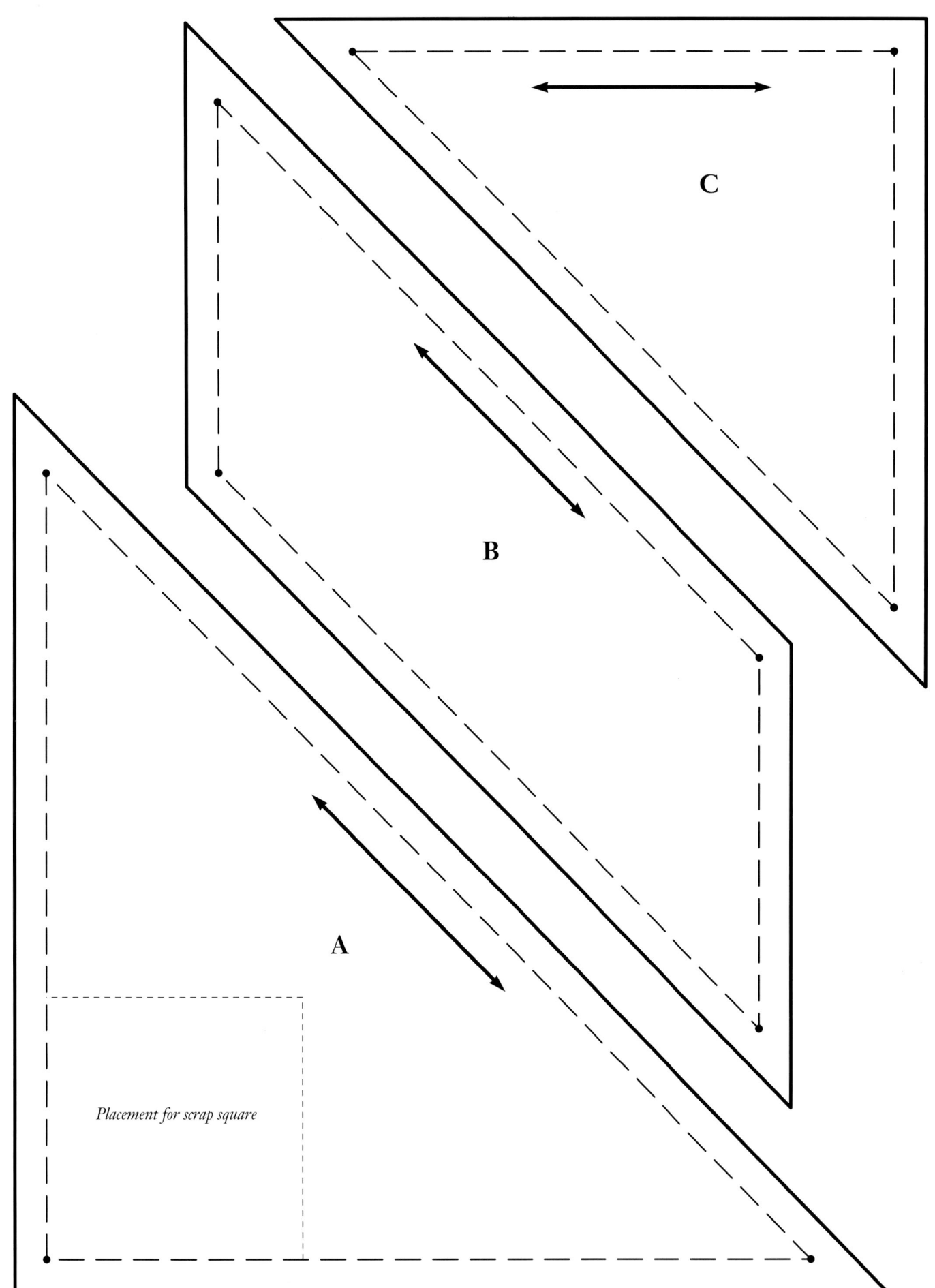

29

Quilt by Becky Olson Johnson
Badger, Minnesota

Roads

Becky Johnson made *Roads* as a gift for her nephew, Matthew. "It seemed appropriate for Matthew," Becky says, "because he loves to play with toy cars, and the blue arcs make perfect roads for his vehicles.

Finished Quilt Size
63½" x 95½"

Number of Blocks and Finished Size
60 blocks   8" x 8"

Fabric Requirements
Blue   3¾ yards*
Assorted light
  print   3 yards
Assorted dark
  prints   3 yards
Backing   5¾ yards

*Includes fabric for binding.

Number to Cut**
Template A   60 light prints
               60 dark prints
Template B   60 light prints
               60 dark prints
Template C   120 blue

**See Step 1 to cut borders before cutting other pieces.

Quilt Top Assembly

1. From blue, cut 2 (2¼" x 80½") and 2 (2¼" x 52") border strips. From assorted light prints, cut 54 (3" x 6½") and 4 (3½" x 6½") border strips. From assorted dark prints, cut 54 (3" x 6½") and 4 (3½" x 6½") border strips.

2. Join 1 light print A to 1 dark print A along short edges as shown in **Block Assembly Diagram**. Join 1 light print B to 1 C; join 1 dark print B to 1 C. Join B/C units to As as shown to complete 1 block. Repeat to make 60 blocks.

3. Referring to **Setting Diagram**, join blocks in 10 rows of 6 blocks each. Be careful to orient each block as shown to create the "road" pattern. Join rows.

4. Join 2¼" x 80½" blue border strips to sides of quilt top. Join 2¼" x 52" blue border strips to top and bottom edges of quilt top, butting corners.

5. To make 1 pieced side border, join 31 (3" x 6½") print strips along long edges, alternating dark and light prints as shown in **Setting Diagram** and photograph. Join 1 (3½" x 6½") print strip to each end of pieced border. Repeat to make second side border. Join pieced borders to sides of quilt top.

To make top pieced border, join 23 (3" x 6½") print strips along long edges, alternating dark and light prints. Join 1 (3½" x 6½") print strip to each end of pieced border. Repeat to make bottom border. Join pieced borders to top and bottom edges of quilt top, butting corners.

Quilting
Quilt each seam in-the-ditch, or quilt as desired.

Finished Edges
Referring to instructions on page 11, make 10 yards of 2"-wide bias or stright-grain binding from blue. Apply binding to quilt edges.

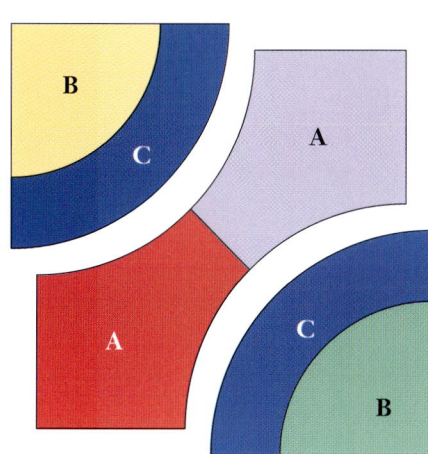

Block Assembly Diagram

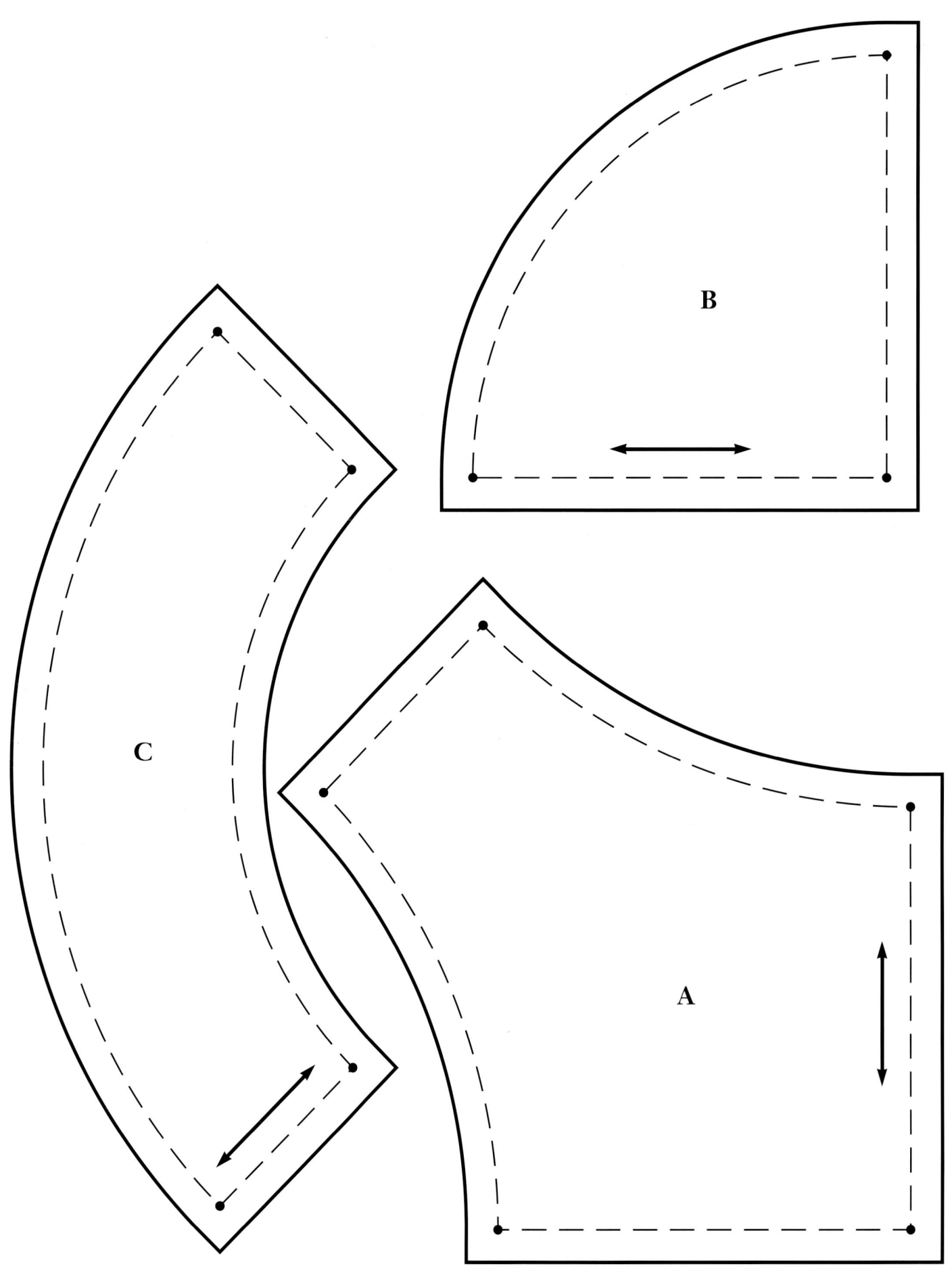

Quilt by Dr. Marianna Frost
Calvert, Texas

Memory Chain

Memory Chain is Marianna Frost's adaptation of a traditional pattern she has had since the 1960s. To unify the scraps, Marianna chose a print of teddy bears on a green background to use for the repeating squares on point. "The colors are *not* placed randomly," she says. "I try to place each fabric next to a piece with a similar or complementary color. Then I always use a lot of red for drama!"

Finished Quilt Size
73" x 88½"

Number of Blocks and Finished Size
90 blocks   7½" x 7½"

Fabric Requirements
Green   2¾ yards*
Muslin   3½ yards
Dark print   ¾ yard**
Light and medium
    scraps   3¾ yards
Backing   5½ yards

*Includes fabric for binding.

**Marianna chose a conversation print and centered the teddy-bear motifs in each A.

Number to Cut
Template A   45 dark print
Template B   198 muslin
               414 light and medium scraps
Template C   504 light and medium scraps
Template D   180 muslin
Template E   36 muslin

Quilt Top Assembly

1. From green, cut 2 (3½" x 89") and 2 (3½" x 74") border strips.

2. Referring to **Block 1 Assembly Diagram**, join 4 muslin Bs to 1 dark print A. Join scrap Cs together. Join 2 scrap Bs to 1 muslin D and 2 scrap Bs to 1 muslin D reversed. Complete block as shown. Repeat to make 45 Block 1s.

Referring to **Half-Block 1 Assembly Diagram**, join 1 muslin B to 1 scrap B; repeat with 1 more pair of Bs. Join each of these units to a scrap C. Join 1 muslin E and 1 scrap B. Join 1 scrap B to 1 muslin E reversed. Complete Half-Block 1 as shown. Repeat to make 9 Half-Block 1s.

3. Referring to **Block 2 Assembly Diagram**, join 2 scrap Bs to 1 muslin D and 2 scrap Bs to 1 muslin D reversed. Join scrap Cs. Complete Block 2 as shown. Repeat to make 45 Block 2s.

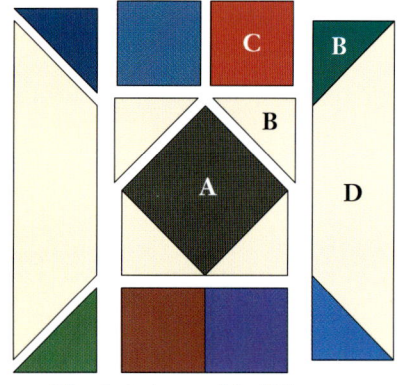
Block 1 Assembly Diagram
Make 45.

Half-Block 1 Assembly Diagram
Make 9.

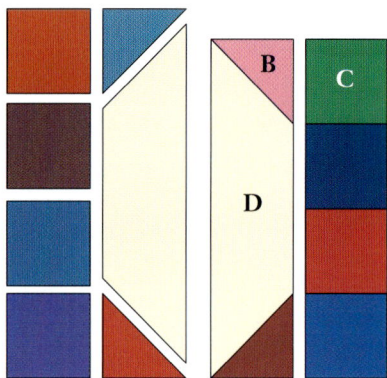
Block 2 Assembly Diagram
Make 45.

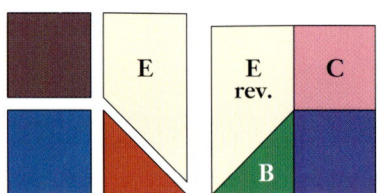
Half-Block 2 Assembly Diagram
Make 9.

Referring to **Half-Block 2 Assembly Diagram**, join 1 scrap B to 1 muslin E and 1 scrap B to 1 muslin E reversed. Join scrap Cs. Complete Half-Block 2 as shown. Repeat to make 9 Half-Block 2s.

4. Referring to **Quilt Top Assembly Diagram**, join 4 Half-Block 1s and 5 Half-Block 2s for Row 1, beginning with Half-Block

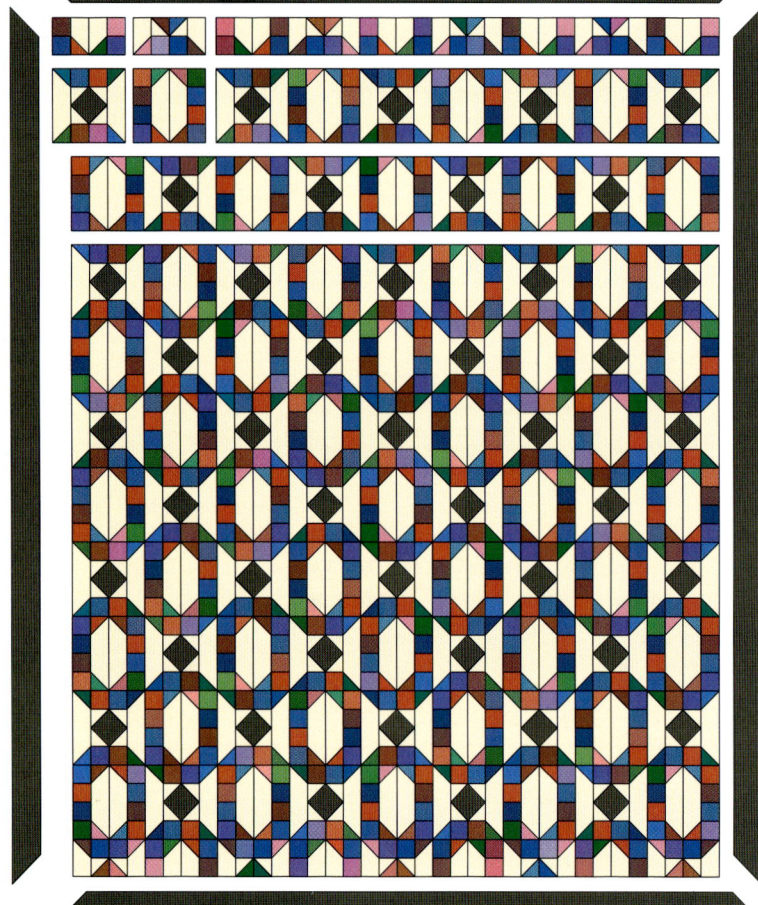
Quilt Top Assembly Diagram

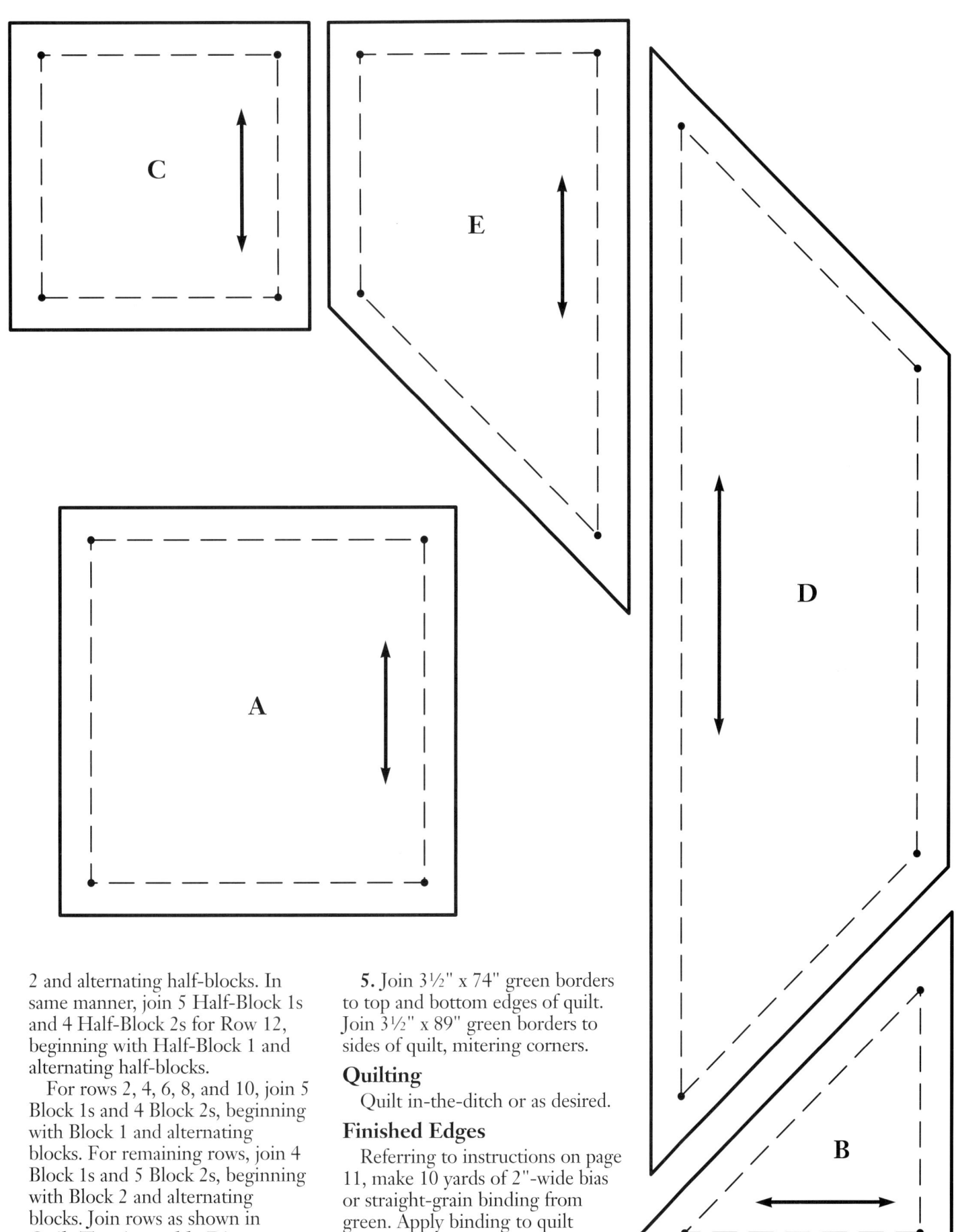

2 and alternating half-blocks. In same manner, join 5 Half-Block 1s and 4 Half-Block 2s for Row 12, beginning with Half-Block 1 and alternating half-blocks.

For rows 2, 4, 6, 8, and 10, join 5 Block 1s and 4 Block 2s, beginning with Block 1 and alternating blocks. For remaining rows, join 4 Block 1s and 5 Block 2s, beginning with Block 2 and alternating blocks. Join rows as shown in **Quilt Top Assembly Diagram**.

5. Join 3½" x 74" green borders to top and bottom edges of quilt. Join 3½" x 89" green borders to sides of quilt, mitering corners.

Quilting
Quilt in-the-ditch or as desired.

Finished Edges
Referring to instructions on page 11, make 10 yards of 2"-wide bias or straight-grain binding from green. Apply binding to quilt edges.

Quilt by Mable Azbill Webb
Jackson, Tennessee

Texas Star

This star pattern, one of many associated with the Lone Star State, was first published in 1928. The scrappy fabrics recall a time when quilts were made from necessity and not just for beauty and pleasure.

Finished Quilt Size
96" x 101⅜"

Fabric Requirements
Muslin	5 yards
Blue print	2⅝ yards
Rose print	2⅞ yards
Assorted prints	5 yards
Assorted solids	1 yard
Backing	9 yards
Fabric for binding	1 yard

Number to Cut*
Template A	68 solids
Template B	424 prints**
Template C	8 prints†
Template C rev.	8 prints†
Template D	8 solids
Template E	227 muslin
Template F	14 prints
Template G	2 prints
Template G rev.	2 prints
Template H	10 muslin

*See Step 1 to cut borders before cutting other pieces.

**Cut 6 Bs from same print for each whole block and 2 Bs from same print for each half-block.

†Cut 1 C and 1 C rev. from same print for each half-block.

Setting Diagram

Quilt Top Assembly

1. From muslin, cut 2 (2½" x 86") and 2 (2½" x 80½") inner borders. From blue print, cut 2 (3½" x 90") and 2 (3½" x 90½") middle borders. From rose print, cut 2 (3½" x 100") and 2 (3½" x 102½") outer borders.

2. Referring to **Star Assembly Diagram**, make 68 whole blocks. Make 8 half-stars, as shown in **Half Star Assembly Diagram**.

3. Join stars and half-stars in 9 horizontal rows as shown in **Setting Diagram**, filling in Es, Fs, Gs, and Hs where indicated.

4. Referring to **Setting Diagram**, join 2½" x 86" muslin borders to sides of quilt. Join 2½" x 80½" muslin borders to top and bottom edges of quilt, butting corners. Join 3½" x 90" blue print borders to sides of quilt. Join 3½" x 90½" blue print borders to top and bottom edges of quilt, butting corners. Join 3½" x 100" rose print borders to sides of quilt. Join 3½" x 102½" rose print borders to top and bottom edges of quilt, butting corners.

Quilting
Outline-quilt each piece.

Finished Edges
Referring to instructions on page 11, make 11½ yards of 2"-wide bias or straight-grain binding. Apply binding to quilt edges.

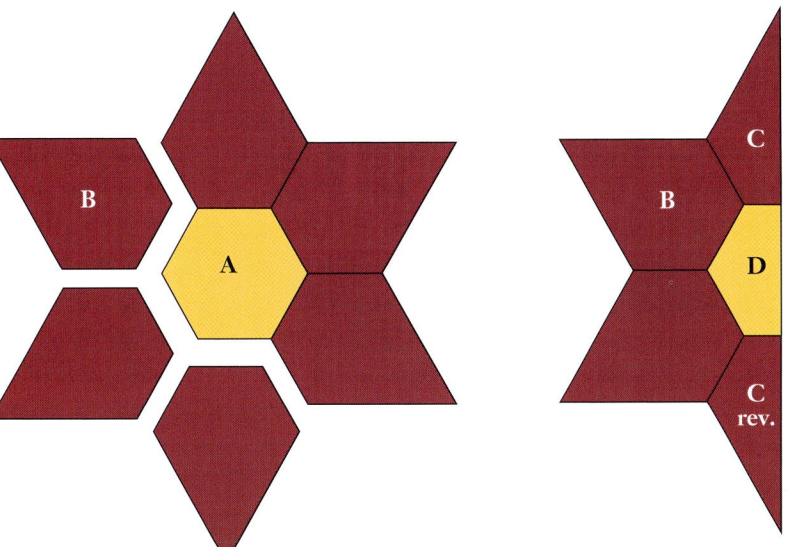

Star Assembly Diagram   **Half-Star Assembly Diagram**

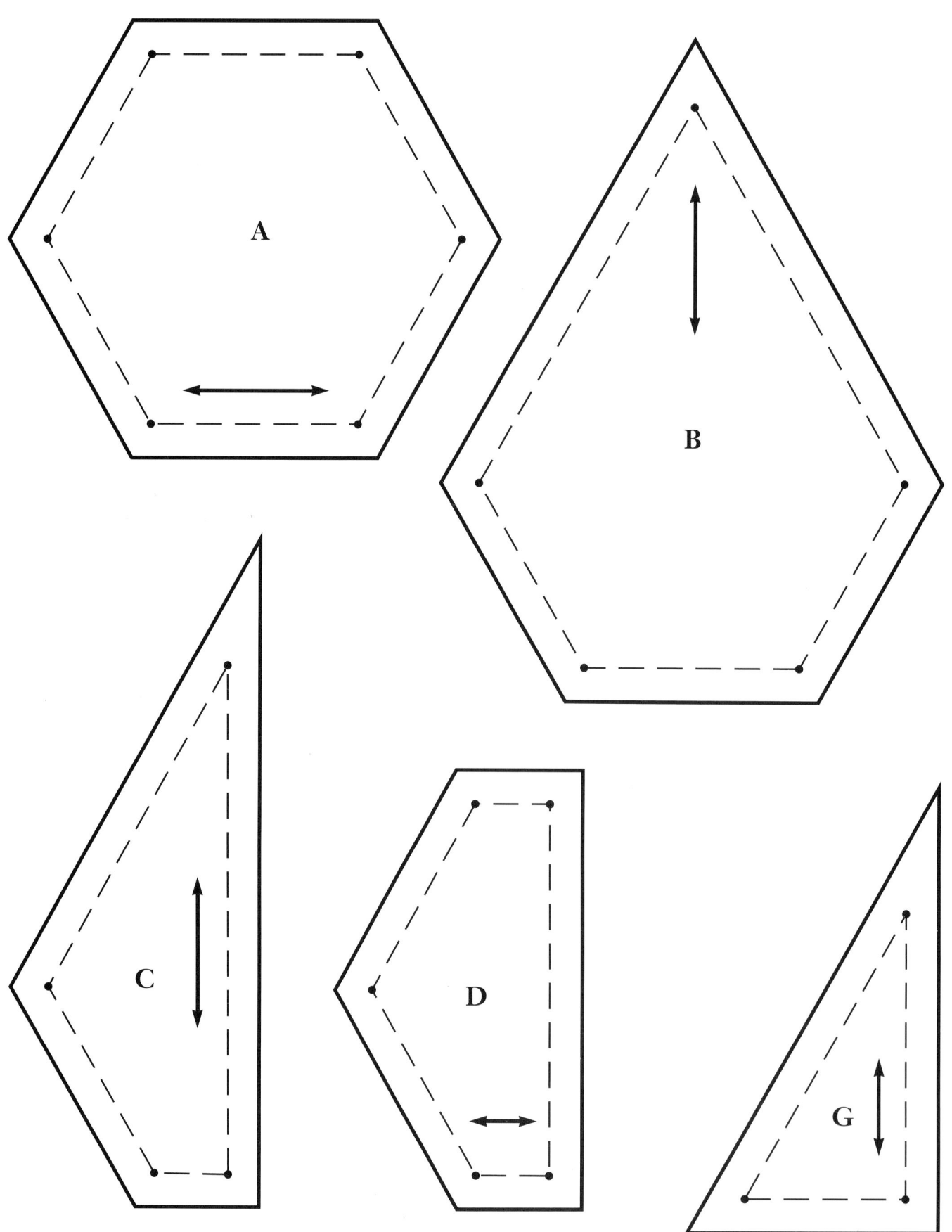

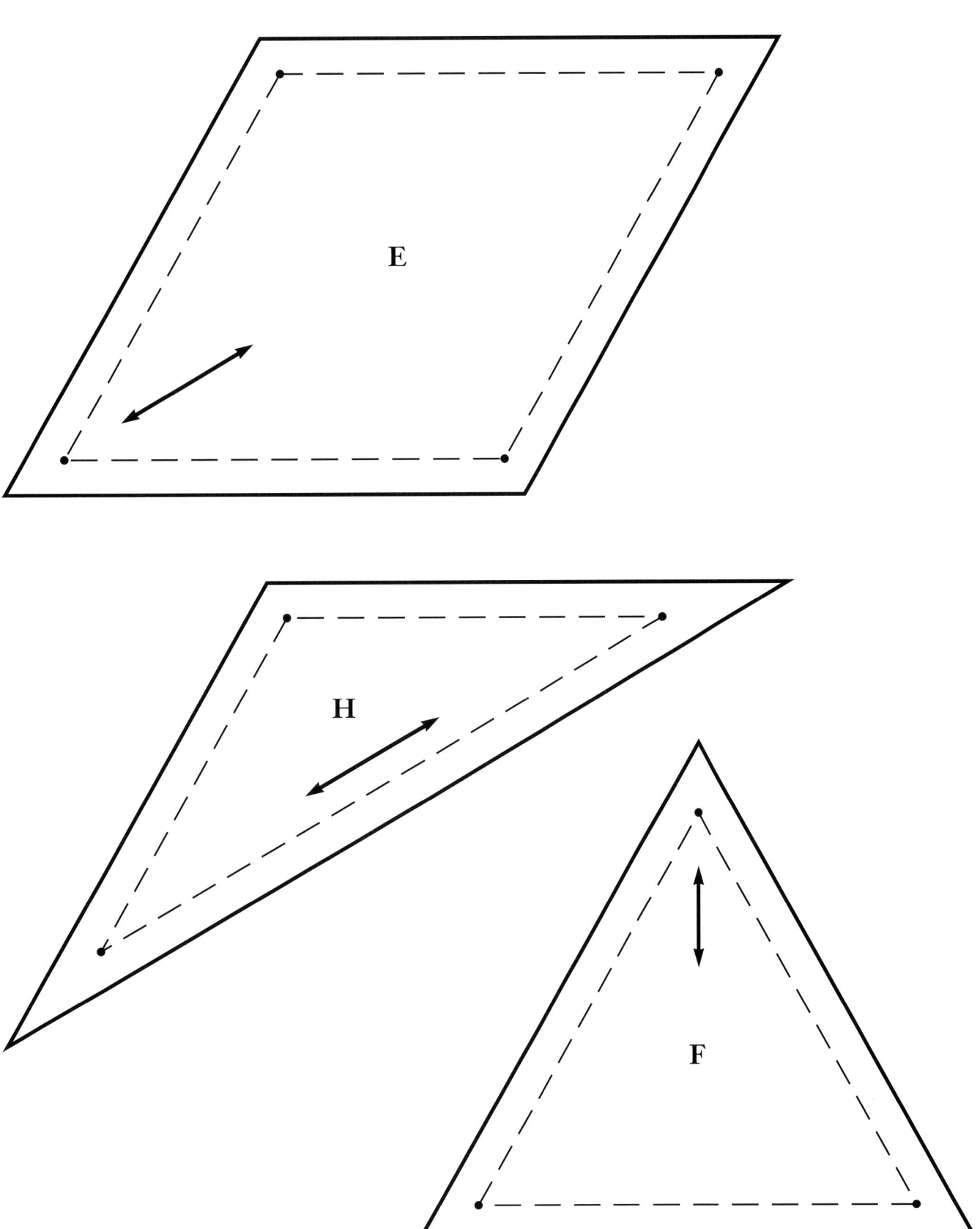

39

Quilt by Birmingham Quilters Guild
Birmingham, Alabama

Maple Leaf

Maple leaves glittering in this salutatory stance remind us throughout the year of the beauty of autumn. In six months Birmingham Quilters Guild members, under the direction of chairperson Martha W. McDonald, hand-pieced blocks, assembled rows of diagonal sashing, and quilted a lattice framework to construct this spectrum of maple-leaf radiance.

Finished Quilt Size
84" x 101"

Number of Blocks and Finished Size
32 blocks 9" x 9"

Fabric Requirements
Scrap prints*
  Brown/rusts ¾ yard
  Yellow/golds ½ yard
  Greens ½ yard
  Red/oranges ½ yard
  Creams ½ yard
Dark green 3⅞ yards
Muslin 2¼ yards
Rust print 4¼ yards**
Backing 5¾ yards

*Total scrap yardage for a Maple Leaf block is a 4" x 24" rectangle.

**Includes fabric for binding.

Number to Cut
Template A 33 brown/rusts
  21 yellow/golds
  21 greens
  12 red/oranges
  9 creams
  64 muslin
Template B 44 brown/rusts
  28 yellow/golds
  28 greens
  16 red/oranges
  12 creams
  128 muslin
Template C 11 brown/rusts
  7 yellow/golds
  7 greens
  4 red/oranges
  3 creams

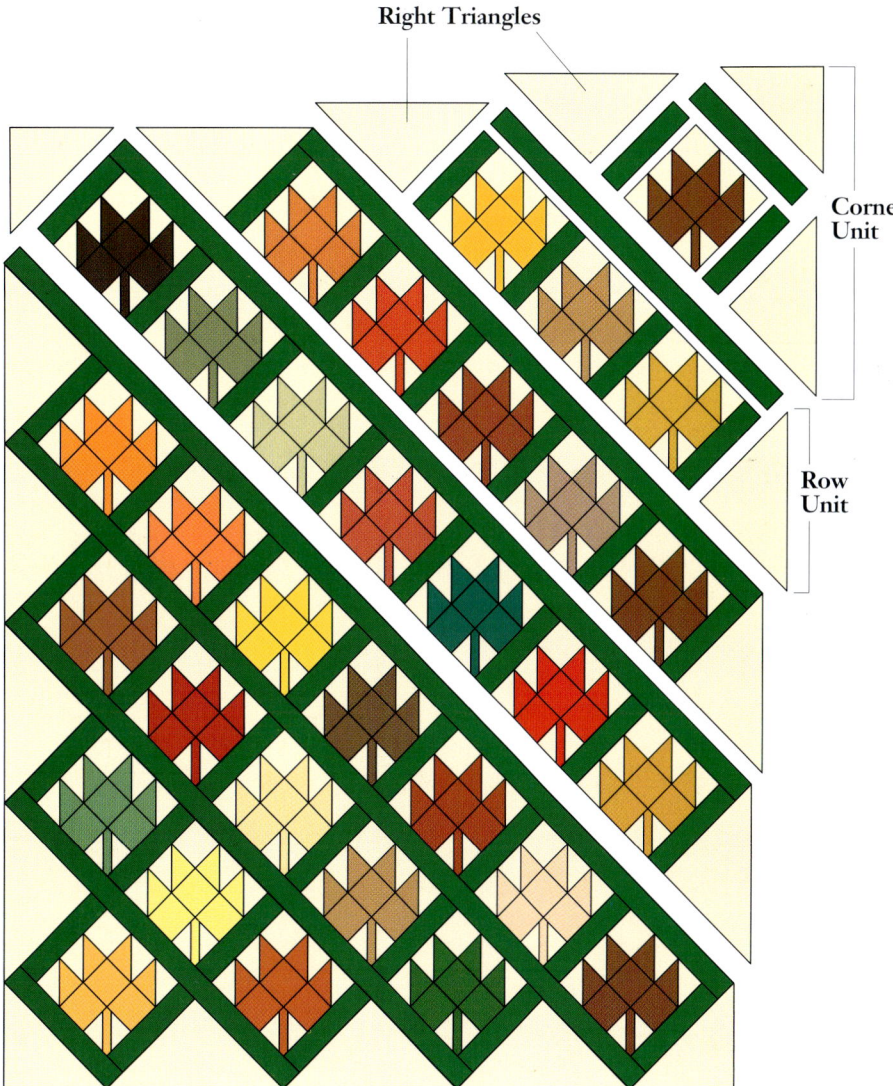

Setting Diagram

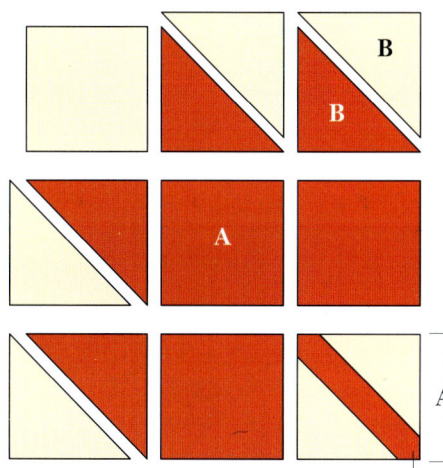

Block Assembly Diagram

Quilt Top Assembly

1. From dark green, cut 9 (2½"-wide) and 40 (2½" x 9½") sashing strips. Also cut 4 (4½"-wide) strips for borders. From rust print, cut 4 (6½"-wide) border strips.

2. Referring to pattern, appliqué 1 C to 1 muslin A. Join scrap print Bs with muslin Bs, as shown in **Block Assembly Diagram.** Join pieced squares with As to form 3 rows. Join rows to make 1 block. Make 32 Maple Leaf blocks.
Note: To save time, string-piece all muslin Bs to scrap Bs. Set aside, and use them as needed for each block.

3. Arrange Maple Leaf blocks in diagonal rows as shown in **Setting Diagram**.

4. Join (2½" x 9½") sashing strips to opposite sides of each Maple Leaf block to form rows, as shown in **Setting Diagram**.

5. Join long dark green sashing strip to 1 side of each block row, as shown in **Setting Diagram**. (The longest sashing strip will be joined to rows at the final assembly of the quilt top.)

6. Cut 4 (16¾") squares from muslin. Cut squares diagonally to form 14 side triangles (you'll have

41

2 extra triangles). Referring to **Setting Diagram**, join 1 triangle to each end of block rows to form row units. (Do not join to corners.)

Cut 2 (10") squares from muslin and cut diagonally to form 4 triangles for corners. Join 2 corner units as shown in **Setting Diagram**. Save remaining 2 triangles for opposite corners.

7. Begin with corner unit and join rows as shown in **Setting Diagram**. Join 2 remaining corner triangles to remaining corners.

8. Join dark green border strips to quilt, mitering corners.

9. Join rust print border strips to quilt, mitering corners.

Quilting

Outline-quilt along seam lines of Maple Leaf block. Quilt a 1" cross-hatching pattern on large muslin triangles. Quilt parallel diagonal lines at a 45° angle, 3½" apart, on green and rust print borders.

Finished Edges

Referring to instructions on page 11, make 11 yards of 2"-wide bias or straight-grain binding from rust print. Apply binding to quilt edges.

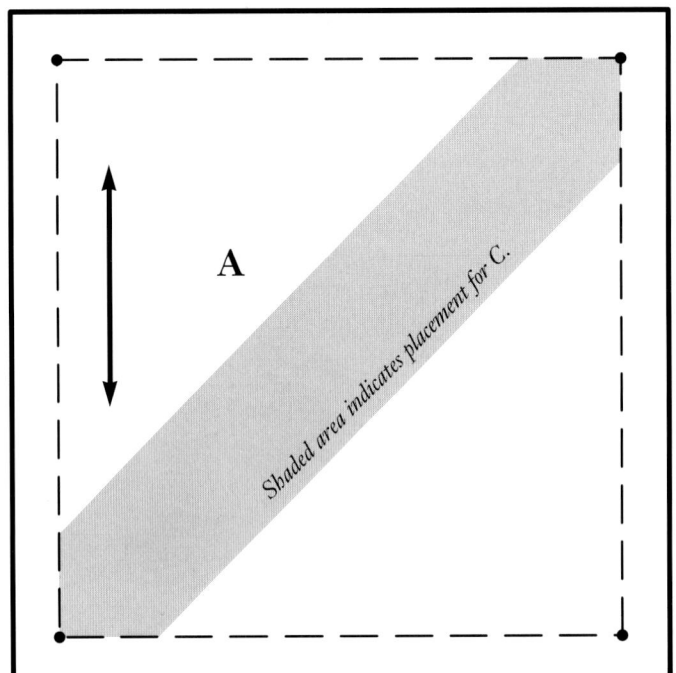

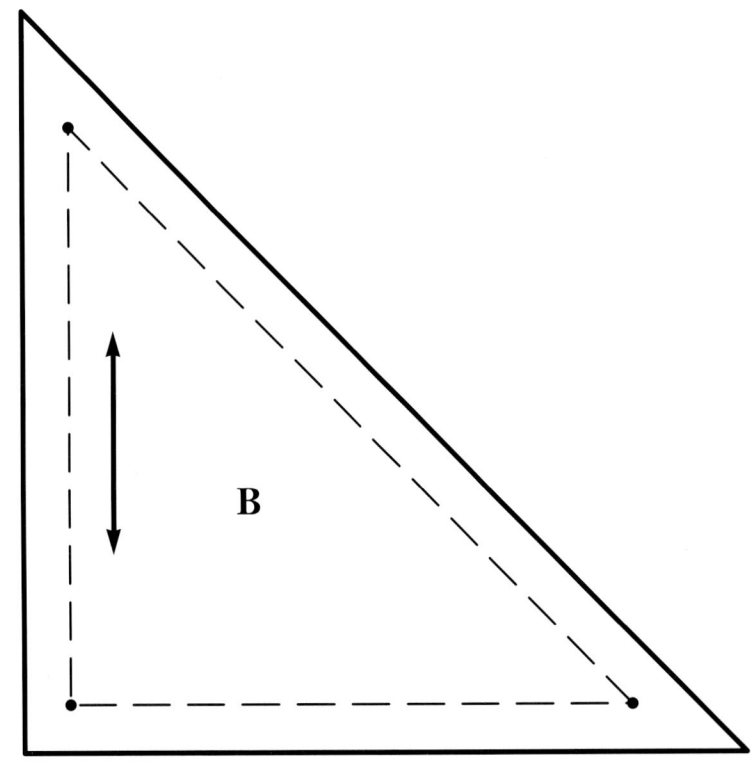

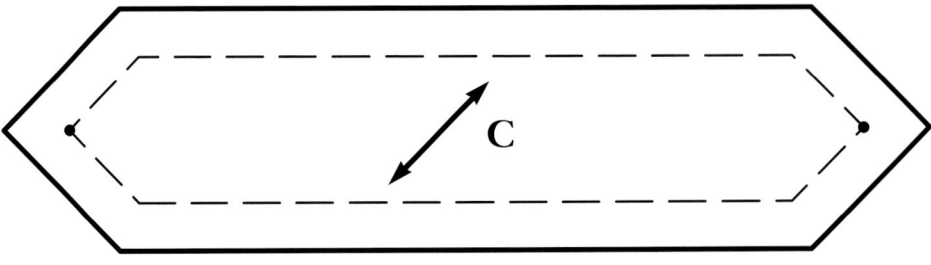

Quilt by Ilse Perea
Greenville, South Carolina

Wandering Star

The star pattern shows up in more American quilts than any other design. Before the arrival of printed patterns, quilters developed their star designs by folding squares of paper and then drawing diamonds within the fold lines. The most popular one, the eight-pointed star, has more variations than any other.

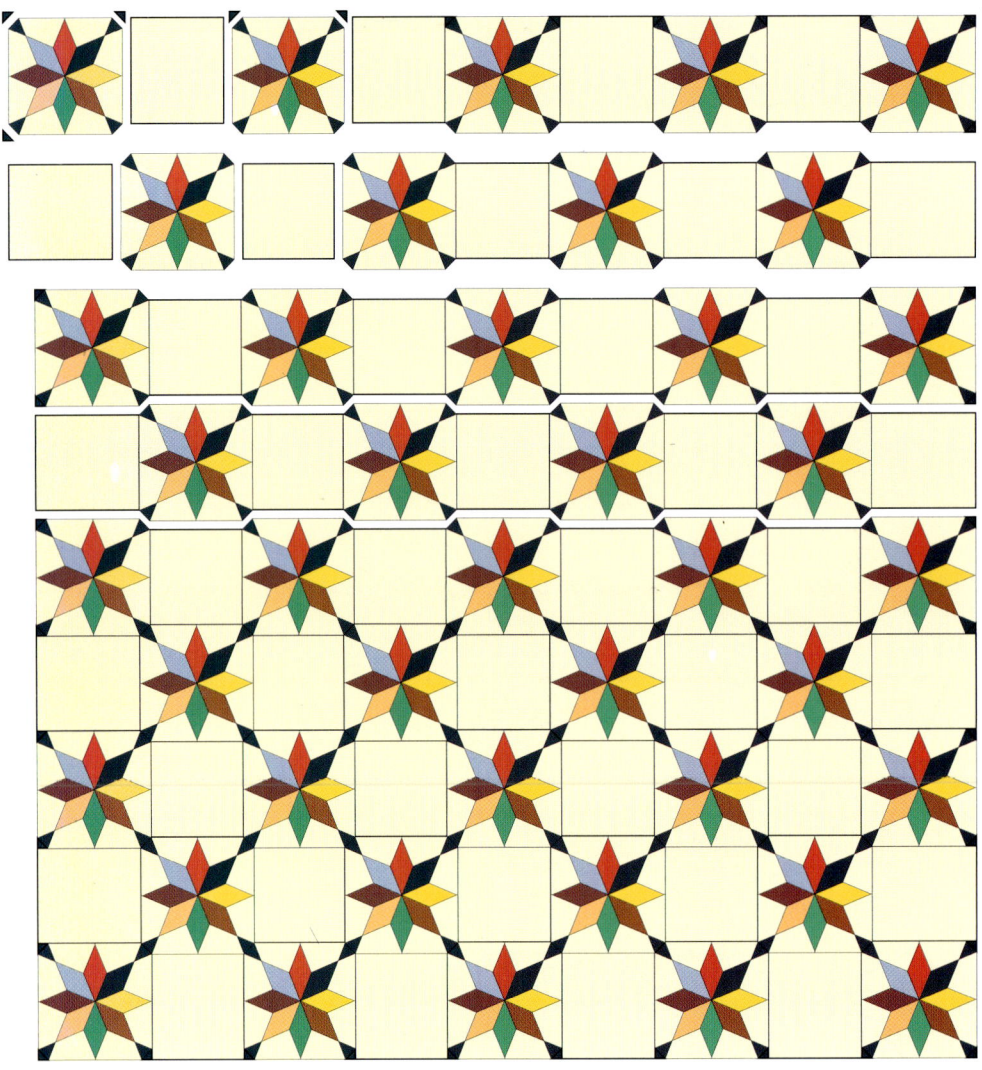

Setting Diagram

Finished Quilt Size
98" x 98"

Number of Blocks and Finished Size
41 blocks   10⅞" x 10⅞"

Fabric Requirements
White	6¾ yards
Assorted prints	5½ yards
Black print	2½ yards*
Backing	9 yards

*Includes 1 yard for binding.

Number to Cut
Template A	328 prints
Template B	164 white**
Template B rev.	164 white**
Template C	164 black print
Template D	36 black print

**See Step 1 to cut setting squares and side rectangles before cutting other pieces.

Quilt Top Assembly

1. From white, cut 24 (9½") setting squares. Also from white, cut 16 (9½" x 10½") side rectangles. Set aside.

2. Referring to **Block Assembly Diagram**, make 41 star blocks.

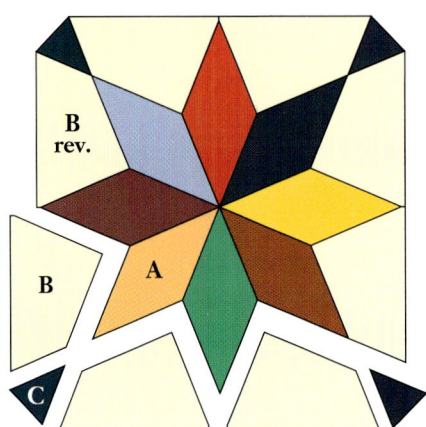

Block Assembly Diagram

Refer to page 6, Step 8, for tips on sewing set-in seams.

3. Referring to **Setting Diagram**, add additional Ds to outside blocks as shown. Join star blocks, white setting squares, and side rectangles in horizontal rows as shown. Join rows.

Quilting
Outline-quilt each block. Refer to photograph to quilt a spider web in the setting squares and the side rectangles.

Finished Edges
Referring to instructions on page 11, make 11 yards of 2"-wide bias or straight-grain binding from black print. Apply binding to quilt edges.

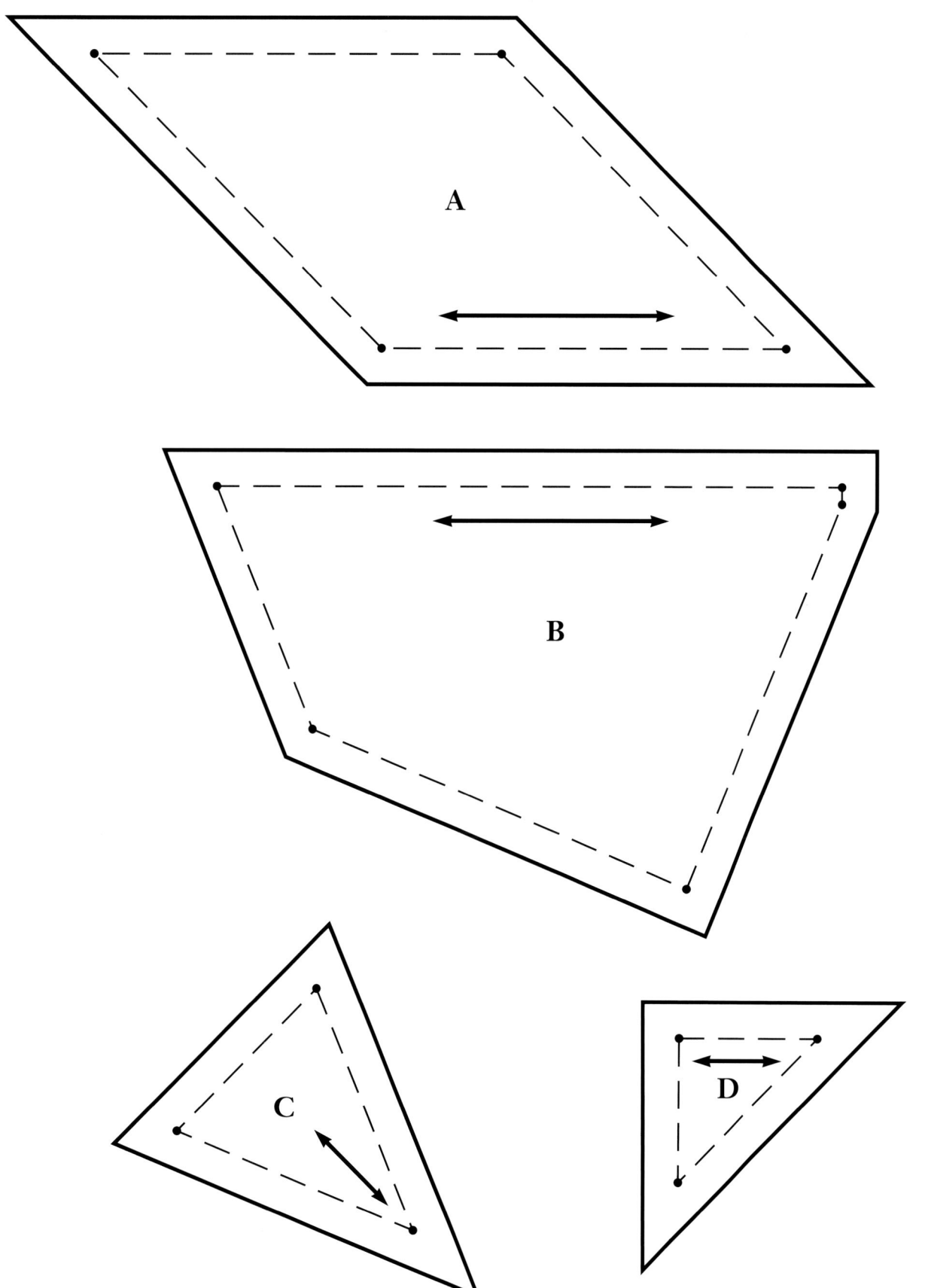

45

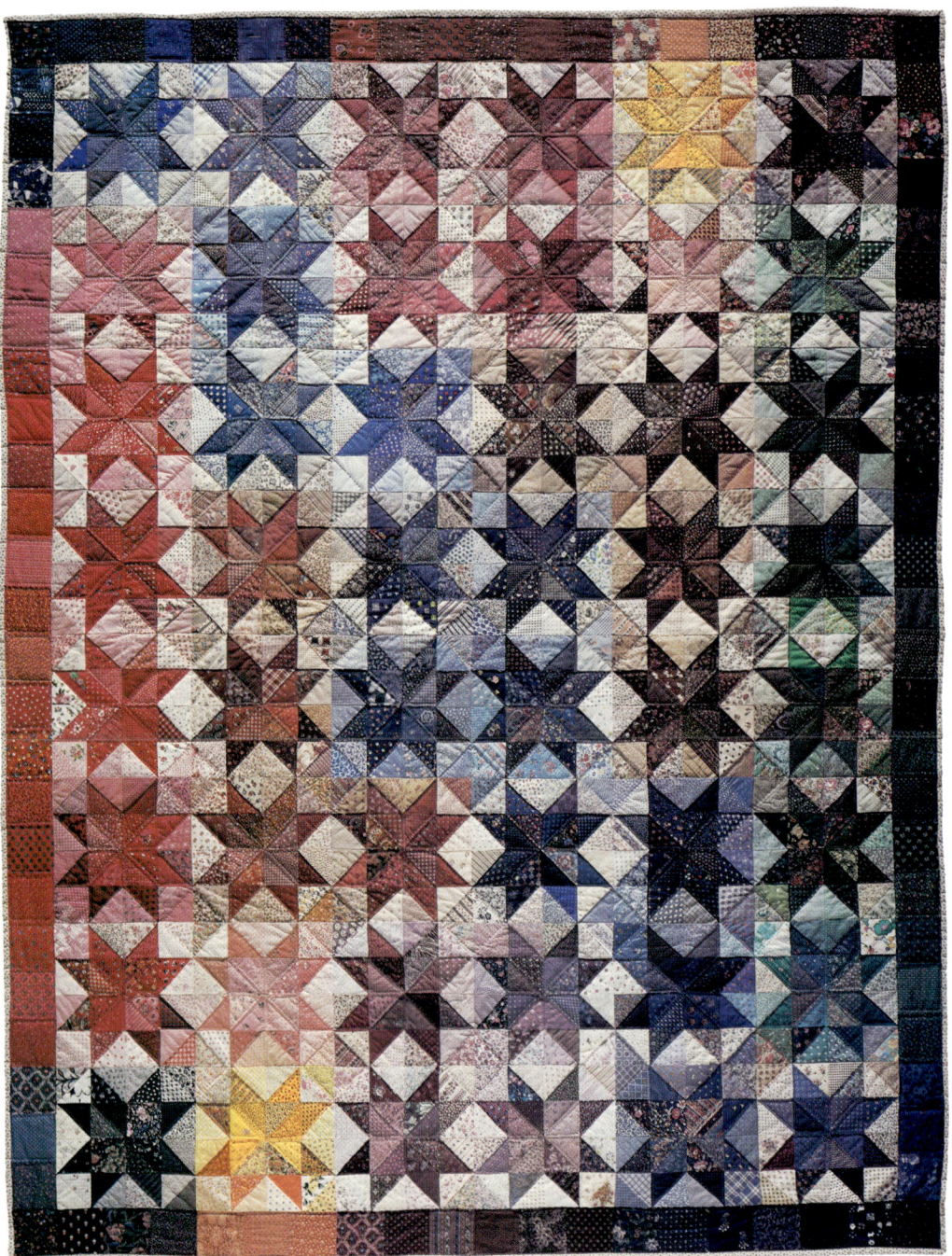

*Quilt by Lorraine Vignoli
Commack, New York*

My Charming Star

Charm quilts, in which no two pieces are cut from the same fabric, first became popular around the turn of the century. Lorraine Vignoli placed an ad in a quilt magazine inviting readers to participate with her in a fabric swap. The fabrics in her quilt are the results of these swaps. All were collected from charm traders in the United States, England, and Australia.

Finished Quilt Size
80" x 104"

Number of Blocks and Finished Size
48 blocks   12" x 12"

Fabric Requirements
Scraps of 1,624 different fabrics
Backing   6 yards
Fabric for
  binding   1 yard

Number to Cut
Template A   768 light
    768 dark
Template B   88 assorted

Quilt Top Assembly
1. Referring to **Block Assembly Diagram**, make 48 blocks.
2. Referring to **Setting Diagram**, join blocks in 8 horizontal rows of 6 blocks each. Join rows.
3. Join 24 Bs for each side border. Join 20 Bs each for top and bottom borders. Join side borders to quilt. Join borders to top and bottom edges of quilt.

Quilting
Outline-quilt each star point in blocks and each B in border.

Finished Edges
Referring to instructions on page 11, make 10½ yards of 2"-wide bias or straight-grain binding. Apply binding to quilt edges.

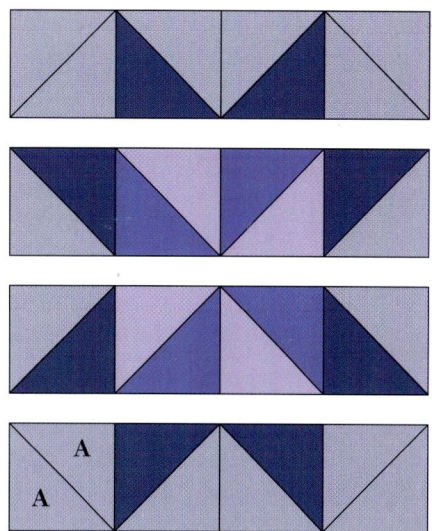

Block Assembly Diagram

Setting Diagram

47

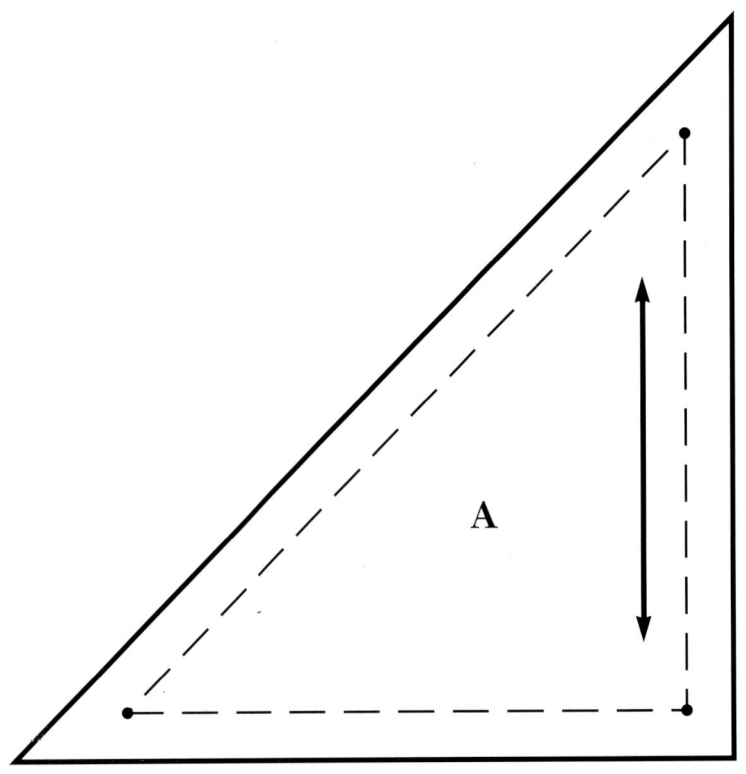
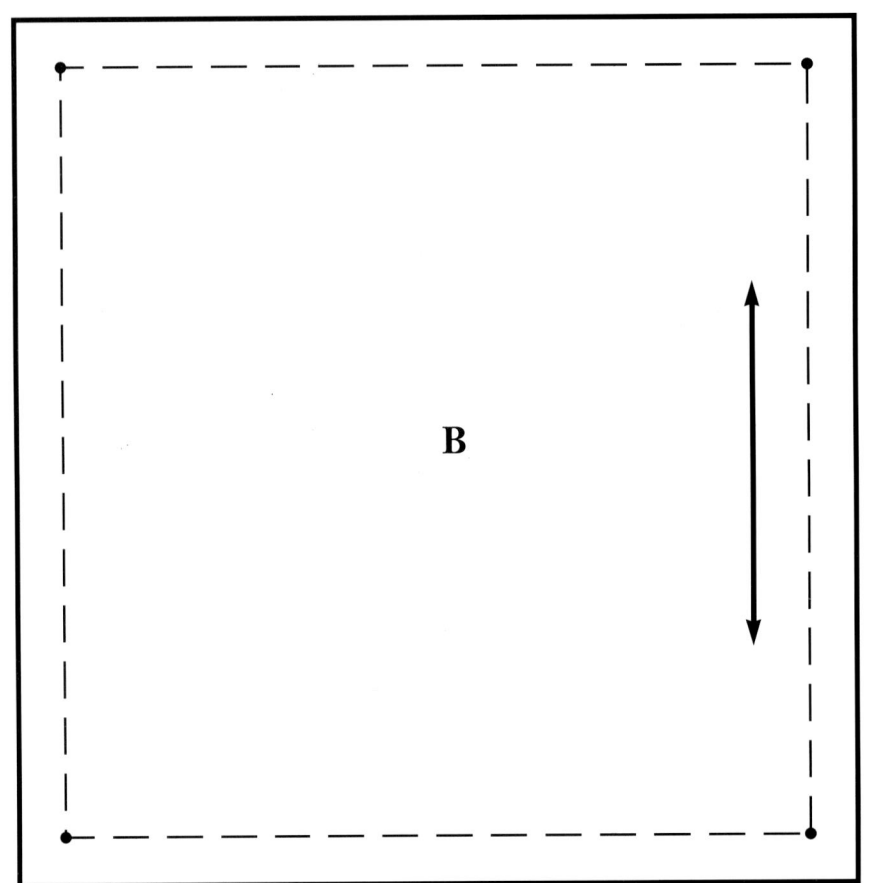